'In this moving and spellbinding medi[illegible] remorse, Kate Rossmanith shuttles betw[illegible] personal reminiscences as she traces out the repercussions of the "calamitous mistakes and misfortunes" that haunt our everyday lives. This is the gift Rossmanith gives her readers: through her elegant prose and riveting story structure, she opens up an elusive subject for us to ponder, withholding obvious closure, and yet satisfying us that she has reached the heart of the matter. Rarely does a book enter a reader's life so completely.'

MICHAEL JACKSON, author of
The Varieties of Temporal Experience

SMALL WRONGS

KATE ROSSMANITH

HOW WE REALLY SAY SORRY IN LOVE, LIFE AND LAW

hardie grant books

Published in 2018 by Hardie Grant Books,
an imprint of Hardie Grant Publishing

Hardie Grant Books (Melbourne)
Building 1, 658 Church Street
Richmond, Victoria 3121

Hardie Grant Books (London)
5th & 6th Floors
52–54 Southwark Street
London SE1 1UN

hardiegrantbooks.com

NATIONAL LIBRARY OF AUSTRALIA
A catalogue record for this book is available from the National Library of Australia

Small Wrongs
ISBN 9781743794111

10 9 8 7 6 5 4 3 2 1

Cover design by Sandy Cull
Typeset by Cannon Typesetting
Printed by McPherson's Printing Group, Maryborough, Victoria

FSC www.fsc.org MIX Paper from responsible sources FSC® C001695

The paper this book is printed on is certified against the Forest Stewardship Council® Standards. FSC promotes environmentally responsible, socially beneficial and economically viable management of the world's forests.

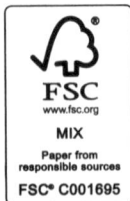

To my family

Remorse is memory awake.

Emily Dickinson

I

COURTROOM APPEARANCES

1

The first court case I ever observed belonged to a woman guilty of murder. She had deliberately run over a young man with her car. I had followed news reports of the trial, for the story seemed so strange, and had seen grainy CCTV footage: the vehicle lunging at the 21-year-old who darts out of its way; the car reversing and charging once more, striking him, thrusting him underneath.

Anyone can attend court. You scan the court lists, locate the case you are looking for. You can also slip into hearings about which you know nothing. The public is allowed to be there, but it never feels that way, and you keep expecting someone to ask you to leave. The criminal courts are open secrets. Raw lives, with all their calamitous mistakes and misfortunes, are laid bare.

The façade of the New South Wales Supreme Court building was what I'd expected – sandstone arches and high tradition – but its foyer was in want of repair. The walls had cavities where the plaster had come away, as if bitten into by an animal, and on the sweeping staircase, a structure fit for the arrival of a princess, masking tape held a banister knob steady. The security machine at the courtroom entrance looked like space-age gear in a Victorian relic.

People gathered outside Courtroom 3 for the sentencing proceedings. Mostly they were dressed in jeans and t-shirts, law students freed from classrooms and sent to study real life. Among them was a pinched-looking woman in her late fifties with peroxided hair in the style of a firework that reminded me of David Bowie. She was the offender's mother. Her 39-year-old daughter was somewhere below us in the bowels of this place, waiting to walk up the stairs into court and natural light.

We filed in. I took a seat at the back and listened to the reverberating procession as the crowd filled the room.

A student near me didn't know what this case concerned.

'What is this case?' she asked someone next to her.

'This is a very serious case,' the onlooker replied. 'A woman has been convicted of murder. Today is her sentencing hearing.'

'Oh.'

'Go up to someone afterwards and ask about it. Speak to the prosecutor. She's lovely. You won't understand anything today unless you ask.'

The prosecutor did look lovely: a slender brunette with the high-wattage smile of a party host. During the trial, she had won over the twelve most important people in the room and they'd returned a finding in her favour. Today the prosecution and defence would present evidence to the judge that would help determine the length and nature of the offender's sentence. The woman would be sentenced for murder, that was a given, but precisely how many years she would serve, and what her non-parole period would be, was for the judge to decide. The sentencing itself wouldn't happen for another fortnight.

I hadn't been at the trial. It wasn't the defendant's guilt or innocence that interested me so much as what was to be done with her once her guilt was established. Even at that early point I knew that jury trials aren't what the criminal justice system is about. They are rare in Australia. Mostly people plead guilty.

A man and a woman shuffled into a row behind the prosecutor. I recognised them from the news as the victim's father and mother: him thin and shrunken, her with the ghostly pallor of a person not quite there. Then the brother arrived. I heard him before I saw him, the *thud thud thud* of weighty feet on the old floor. Tall and wide, he squeezed between his parents. The row was designed for three, however he had the bulk of two people, and rolled his shoulders to fit.

I waited for the offender to emerge, but she already had. Unaccustomed to the staging of court proceedings, I'd missed her unceremonious entrance not through a door but from a staircase below that coughed her up from nowhere. It took me minutes to register that the lonely figure who'd materialised at a bench to my left was the woman herself. She could have been a court reporter, anyone, were it not for her form. She was terribly contracted. Head bowed and sobbing softly, blonde hair drooped around her face, she wrapped her arms and hands tightly around her stomach. Dabbing her eyes with a screwed-up tissue, she slid glances at her mother with the firework hair.

The elderly judge entered, dressed in scarlet, looking like Christmas. He spent fifteen minutes silently reading the submissions from the lawyers while the rest of us tried not to fidget. Then the prosecutor made mention of documents or legislation, the substance of which I couldn't catch. This sentencing hearing was similar to most others I would come to sit in on: preliminary to the offender being formally sentenced, it comprised muted, heady conversations between legal counsel and the judge. But this one was to include testimony from the victim's family.

The young man's mother was called to the witness box to deliver the family's victim impact statement. She approached the front without the usual agency of a conscious individual, as if something else was guiding her there. She began reading the statement and I couldn't make sense of its genre, it being both a celebration of her son's life and a meditation on agony. As this mother spoke – 'Our dear younger son has been murdered', 'The day of his funeral was the most harrowing day of our lives', 'The first shovel of dirt hit the coffin with a loud crack: we reeled in horror' – people in the room wept, including the woman in the dock who kept tugging the edges of her black suit jacket towards her middle as if the fabric alone was preventing her insides from spilling out.

Weeks earlier, a jury had reached its verdict. It had accepted the Crown's version of events: that early on a June morning in 2008 outside a 7-Eleven store on Sydney's north shore, the woman got into a trivial argument with the 21-year-old boy, his brother and some friends during which time the boy had thrown cheeseballs at her car; that she was drunk, on drugs and driving without a licence; and that, enraged and humiliated, she stalked him with her car and used it as a weapon as she crashed down a set of steps with the young man trapped underneath. The woman always accepted responsibility for his death but she had pleaded guilty to the lesser charge of manslaughter, insisting that she had not intended to drive at him, that her passenger (who was never charged) had taken control of the wheel and that it had been a tragic accident.

That day at the sentencing hearing, I could not know the woman's exact feeling but I was certain of her pain. Like the boy's family – the father and brother trembling with grief in the front row as the mother spoke of their trauma – she appeared to be distressed. It was, however, a different order of misery. The victim's family was wild with it. There was a palpable, bursting rage to their grief. So when the woman's lawyer engaged the judge in a detached debate as to the 'objective seriousness' of the murder – was the murder at the more serious or less serious end of the scale? – it was not unexpected that the boy's father rushed from the courtroom white with shock, while the brother, that colossal front-rower of a man, jumped to his feet yelling 'Fuck you! Fuck you!' to the lawyer and roared out behind his father. The family was so thick with despair that the outburst felt inevitable. Compared to them, the woman's ache looked smaller. There was no fury in it. Hers seemed ashamed, fearful, a tight sort of a thing.

*

Afterwards I kept thinking about that woman. It was as if her buckled body was a theatrical *gestus*, a pure, physical manifestation of a plagued psyche. Her lawyer had argued that she was remorseful and that this should be taken into account. It now fell to the judge to determine whether or not she really was.

To me, it seemed a puzzle of theatre and the law. The question of bodies and emotion – how we furnish ourselves with feeling and how others recognise it on us – had long preoccupied me, and perhaps performance was somewhere at its core. As an undergraduate at the University of Sydney, I studied Philosophy and English Literature and learnt something of the nature of being and of Shakespeare's stage, and I performed in student productions including *Electra*. I loved reciting scripts, listening to other people's voices cut in and out, but I was no good at acting. I couldn't consciously coordinate my body with how I felt or tried to feel.

At university I also wrote a doctoral thesis in Performance Studies, which was a discipline born of a marriage in the 1960s between theatre and anthropology, and one not only interested in opera, theatre, dance, but in other categories of performance too. I read about rituals and spectacles, about weddings and funeral rites, and about ceremonial displays of mourning. I learnt how satirists in ancient Rome saw humans as role-players and social existence as a performance, and I read the work of twentieth-century sociologists and anthropologists who analysed how we perform social roles in everyday life. For them, the metaphor of 'performance' was not meant to suggest our conduct is contrived – although sometimes it may be – but rather to examine customs and expressive behaviour. I read how the eighteenth-century neo-classicists attached the term 'theatre' to the act of gazing: how, for them, the word encompassed a looking out at, or into, the world.

I also learnt that, for at least 500 years, people have used the language of theatre to describe trial courts. Audiences recognised theatrical features – costuming, staging, ritualised actions – but mostly the two things have been linked pejoratively: the trial is about solemn truth; the theatre is artifice and entertainment. In court we study people and discredit those thought to be performing. And yet at the same time, courtroom processes involve, and in some cases demand, enactments from people.

The courts are, or can be, theatres of remorse. That woman in the dock, for instance, seemed riddled with it, although it would be many more weeks before I would learn for certain what the judge thought.

In the years after that woman's case, I became a spectator, examining how people comport themselves. Then I spoke with them, asking them what they thought remorse was and what they wanted it to do. I visited offices and homes and interviewed lawyers, forensic physicians, caseworkers, victims; and I met with offenders and with the people whose job it was to judge them. I watched and took notes, collecting stories of courtroom sorrow and punishment, forgiveness and atonement.

The university where I worked was pleased. I was doing something called 'original research' that would yield 'new knowledge'. This was my job as an academic: to be curious about the world, to study new things, or old things in new ways, and to disseminate findings. I had learnt of an anomaly in the criminal law. In many legal jurisdictions of the world, including in the USA, England, Canada and Australia, an offender's remorse is a mitigating factor at sentence, with judges legally obliged to take it into account. And yet how judges evaluated such expressions was unclear. My study would help society better understand the ways in which the courts assessed contrition.

They say that researchers are driven by curiosity. I pretended I was. I pretended I could examine remorse as if it were a plant or a dead mouse, probing it under a microscope, listing its properties and potential for reparation. Curiosity is aloof, cerebral. Curiosity can be quelled with explanation. To be curious about a thing is to be detached from it, as if you – the human researcher – and it – the object of inquiry – were unjoined.

2

My father was gardening once when a thorn lodged so deeply in his hand that he required surgery to extract it. He had been cutting back a palm fern that was spilling onto our property from a neighbour's yard. As he tugged and hacked at the fanned leaves he didn't notice the long needles underneath. A spine penetrated his middle finger near the joint, breaking off.

Dad was a university scientist, which meant that, for our family, nature and natural forces were not plain givens but phenomena to marvel at. He called us over, telling us of the plant's spikes and how one was hidden in his finger, showing us the entry point on his skin. We were little, my siblings and I, at ages when selves are still forming, children yet to separate from their parents, yet to coolly observe them. I stared at his poor hand, alarmed that the outside world could burrow itself so thoroughly into a person. My mother drove him to the clinic. He was given a local anaesthetic, administered via a nerve in his shoulder region, after which he felt an electrical pulse shoot down his arm, causing it to turn numb and become heavy and sausage-like. When it came time for the incision, Dad did not fixate on the sterile white ceiling, as anyone else would have. He remained alert, curious, examining his opened finger and the entire procedure as the doctor poked, pulled and sliced through flesh.

This memory of the thorn, and of my father's mettle, his capacity to study his own insides as if they did not belong to him, impressed itself upon me three decades later when I was afflicted with insomnia.

My husband and I were renting a flat at the headland of a beach in Sydney's east near Bondi. We had moved in together seven years earlier and had straight away reconfigured the dining area into a shared study space, positioning our desks towards the horizon. The apartment was on the top floor of a block of six. It had oversized windows that let in views and that clattered so violently during 'Southerly Busters' we thought they would shatter. The polished floors and poor insulation meant that whenever we argued, the neighbours downstairs shouted at us to shut up.

Our daughter was seventeen months old. I had recently returned part-time from parental leave to my job lecturing and researching at the university in Sydney's north. I was desperate for deep, restorative rest. But night after night, bone-tired by half past eight, I would collapse into bed and lie awake staring into the helpless darkness. When the baby had first arrived, and for many months after, I hadn't slept except for the dizziest of dozing, gripped by an inexplicable panic about which I was still ashamed. But that was when she'd been feeding in the night, and not the twice-a-day breastfeeds I was doing now.

After a week of wakefulness, I decided to wean Jemima. Somewhere I had read that you slumbered better. On a Saturday evening, instead of my giving her the feed, Brad put her to bed while I stood outside in the garden, contemplating the continental parsley and my small grief. Then I went inside and expressed a little milk into the sink. The following morning I again forwent the feed. My body immediately adjusted: there was less and less milk, and then no milk at all. I was shocked at how a ritual to sustaining life could casually vanish.

At night, though, there was no respite.

A doctor gave me sleeping tablets. I lay in bed and felt my limbs grow heavy, attentively thinking happy thoughts as the children do in *Peter Pan*. Sleep wouldn't come. The next night was the same. And the next. Like those of a superhero, my cells overrode whatever chemicals science had assembled to induce unconsciousness.

For weeks I groped for remedies. I quit caffeine, sugar, chilli, nightshades and other stimulating foods. I didn't exercise after midday. I tried meditation. I took sick days from work. I could no longer drive or think.

Then something happened that would take me years to properly understand. In my blurry physical state, I began noticing reports in the newspapers of people's crimes and their remorse. From printed pages, accounts flew at me of judges declaring that offenders' remorse 'could have been more forthcoming', and of courts acknowledging 'genuine apologies' and reducing jail sentences because of them. Some offences were sickening, and I skated over stories of children's death and abuse. Other transgressions were much smaller, simpler. No matter its size, each act and its aftermath would elicit from the judge a comment on remorse or remorselessness.

Haphazardly I kept clippings, stacking them in a dog-eared manila folder. As the paper accumulated, urgent questions hatched about people's ordinary, and extraordinary, entanglements with one another, and about the intimacy of judgment. I wanted to know how you could be sure that a person was truly sorry for what they had done. And I wanted to know what it might mean to climb into the offender's dock and be judged, your failings listed aloud as undisputed facts, your contrition studied for its purity. One morning, with no command of the law, I began pacing the corridors of the criminal courts.

*

Throughout life, people play a subtle game of revelation and concealment with themselves, sneaking glances at what they're made of. Occasionally, though, they are impelled to take a proper look. A psychoanalyst in the 1960s once said that all research involving humans observing other humans should entail tender-minded tough-mindedness, and that what happens *within the observer* must be made known if the nature of what has been observed is ever to be understood.

For as long as I can remember, I have watched the people around me very closely, a quirk I had associated with being the eldest and female: the observant girl taking in her parents' relationship, noting how adults speak, how they move. I began to realise, however, that the reason I watch so closely is because somehow I'd learnt it was risky not to.

When I was seven, we visited family friends who lived in dry bushland in Dural. It was Easter, the sweeping property had no fence, and I wondered how the owners would find their hidden eggs in so much space. Other families were there that day too, and after lunch someone suggested a game of cricket, so a bat and ball were found, and wickets were thumped into the hard ground. I was wicketkeeper. I stood behind a boy not much older than me, with straight hair the colour of straw, who brandished the bat like a sword, before striking the incoming ball, sending it flying. The next ball fell at his feet and dribbled past him. I bent to collect it. As I took my eyes off him and shifted my gaze to the stitched sphere at his ankles, he took a practice swing, flinging the bat backwards. The force of dense wood on my head was strong and sudden and made a cracking noise. I smelt eucalypt and dirt, and people's panic. My cold, iced forehead reconfigured its own contour to include a huge lump that surely couldn't be part of me.

We went to the hospital. I sat in the back of the car between my younger brother and sister, my eyes closed, and begged Dad to drive slowly around every corner and over each bump so that my brain and cranium might stop throbbing. At Royal North Shore, Mum explained to medical staff how it happened. A nurse led me into a separate room. She crouched down and asked me: 'What *really* happened?' As I recounted it – 'ball, boy, bat' – I thought her daft for needing the account twice. X-rays showed my fractured skull.

Not a lot could be done for a broken head, so I spent six weeks at home while the fracture healed. I read books. I slept. I followed Mum on errands. Dark rainbow colours formed around my eyes like an in-built Batgirl mask. One afternoon the boy and his parents arrived with chocolate eggs and apologies. As he announced he was sorry, with the clear diction kids use when they know they are on show, his mum and dad tried not to look horrified upon seeing my face. I ate the peace offering, and that was that.

Social scientists recognise that single incidents (a cricket bat mishap) may lend themselves to story, but are not in themselves responsible for fashioning a human being. A person is formed through historical forces, and through habit. For a writer, the problem with habit – those ordinary, daily sayings and doings around which a child grows up, no one thing sufficiently dramatic to warrant its own plump narrative – is that it disappears through repeated encounters. It eludes reflection until decades later a flurry of feelings revisits you like hiccups.

3

After that woman's sentencing hearing, I had questions to ask a criminal lawyer.

I arrived on the seventh floor of a building on Goulburn Street in the city, which was rented out to legal agencies, including the barrister who had agreed to chat with me. After giving my name at the desk, I watched a young bald man with colourless features lean against the counter and flirt with the receptionist. He was skinny and it seemed he wished he weren't. He jerked his upper body around as if summoning the full weight of a brawny CEO. 'I would have *LAWYER* tattooed to my forehead if someone would put me on a retainer!' he told her. 'I'd want two legal aides. I'd want one murder trial every year, and at least one nasty sexual-assault trial.' She smiled the way women do when what they want to say is, 'You're a fool.' He was dressed in an elegant black suit and the only sign of wear was a deformed left shoe, the back of which was creased because he crushed it with each step.

My interviewee fetched me and we sat in his office with the door closed. On the walls were prints of modern art I didn't recognise, and on his desk was a framed photo, the front of which I couldn't see.

He had spiky hair with gel in it that smelt sweet, and he spoke in a cockney, used-car-salesman accent that sounded parodic.

I asked him what happens when a person is charged, arrested, taken to the police station and allowed to phone their lawyer.

'You're not legally entitled to a phone call,' he said.

'Really?'

'No. That happens in American movies. In Australia it's up to the discretion of the police.'

'Oh. Okay. Let's say you get a call from your client. Do you go down to the station and ask them their version of events?'

'No. I wouldn't ask them that question.'

'Why not?'

'Because they might tell me something that won't help their case,' he said. 'Until I get the brief from the police, it's best for my client to say nothing. I might not want to know their version of events until I see what evidence the police have against them. I do eventually ask my client, "What happened?" but not until I go through the evidence with them to assist them in making a decision as to whether they will plead guilty or not guilty. If the evidence is overwhelming, they would be foolish to defend the charge.'

'So it's not a matter of whether or not they actually committed the offence, but whether or not the evidence is there to prove they did it,' I said.

'Yes,' he said, leaning back in his chair and looking at me down his nose, 'innocent until proven guilty.'

'So, let's say a person pleads guilty. How does the judge assess whether or not they are remorseful?'

'There's no formula,' he said. 'If you have defrauded somebody, you might repay them. If you've killed somebody, you might write letters to the family of *deep* regret and remorse. You might simply say: "Look, I've *done* this and I do not *resile* from the fact that I've done it, and I'm *terribly* sorry." It's as simple as that.'

As he emphasised the words *deep*, *done*, *resile*, *terribly*, he hunched his shoulders and squeezed shut his eyes in the manner of a contrite sports star or politician.

'If someone is remorseful about what they have done,' he continued, 'it stands to reason that they will be less penalised because one assumes they will want to rehabilitate themselves. Other people might deny they've done wrong, or say: "Yeah, I did it, but I couldn't give a rat's arse."'

'Do you talk to your clients about remorse, that it is a mitigating factor and that it would be prudent for them to show some?' I asked.

'No I don't. I possibly invite them to write a letter to the court, or, if it's appropriate, a letter of apology to the victim. There are, of course, people who are *genuinely* remorseful and you know it from the start of the interview because often they are crying.'

'But what precisely about them convinces you they are remorseful?'

'Their behaviour. That they're crying. By speaking to them,' he said.

'But what exactly? When you are sitting opposite someone and they're crying, how do you know if it's distress for themselves or for what they've done?'

'I *don't*. But I'm experienced in *life*. I have *five* children. I've had *numerous* relationships with women. I see criminals day in, day out. Once you've had a bit of experience in life, you can tell whether or not someone is genuinely remorseful.'

Irritated, he told me that, in his line of work, he's 'at the coalface'. Whereas judges are at 'intellectual and analytical' stages of the process, *he's* dealing with 'misery, calamity, fear, mental illness, drug addictions and alcohol'.

'You can *see* if someone is remorseful or not,' he said, picking up a pen and flipping it between his fingers. 'For example, I have a client in custody who has been charged with photographing young boys in the shower. Is he remorseful? Not really, because he doesn't see that what he has done is wrong. He needs to get a psychiatric report because there are underlying issues. His family didn't know about it. He is leading a double life. On the other hand, I see people who are deeply sorry for what they've done. Are they just deeply sorry for the punishment they'll incur? Sometimes that's the case, but I think that if someone is *genuinely* sorry for what they've done, it's evident in what they're prepared to *do*, in what they *say*, to *me*.'

'Do you have an example?' I asked.

'They might say, "Look, I've done this. I'm terribly sorry that I've done this. It's *wrong*, and I shouldn't have done it. I don't know *why* I did it. Maybe it's because I've got an addiction to gambling that I've done this wrong thing and that I've brought shame on my family."'

'Is it as much *how* they say it as *what* they say?'

'Sure. *You* know and *I* know when you see someone who's genuine and when they're not. This isn't rocket science. There's no great mystery here. At the same time, remorse is really difficult to pin down. It's a slippery little sucker.'

'Right,' I said. 'But if remorse is slippery, where does the evidence come from?'

'A person's demeanour in court. Various things. The judge or magistrate will see it. Remorse is not a passive thing. There has to be a demonstration of regret,' he said. 'And sometimes a psychologist will write a pre-sentence report saying, "This person is remorseful." Psychologists use tests. Things outside my realm of understanding.'

'Right.'

Frustrated at what he saw as my deliberate dissatisfaction with his answers, he spun his chair to the computer and searched for the NSW *Crimes (Sentencing Procedure) Act 1999*. He found Section 21A and read it out slowly and loudly: 'Remorse is a mitigating factor "but only if: (i) the offender has provided evidence that he or she has accepted responsibility for his or her actions, and (ii) the offender has acknowledged any injury, loss or damage caused by his or her actions or made reparation for such injury, loss or damage (or both)".'

I knew about this section of the Act. Judges could accept a person's remorse only if there was tangible proof of it. The lawyer hoped that by imperiously announcing it to me, all would be made clear, but we both knew that those four-dozen words weren't going to define remorse, let alone provide a matrix for judges.

It had been almost an hour. He glanced down at his diary to check the next appointment. I quickly thanked him for his time and stood up to leave.

'I've got another five minutes if you want it,' he said. 'In our discussion of remorse, we haven't gotten very far. It seems you haven't really got something to hold onto.'

'No. But I think that's the answer: that I don't have anything to hold onto. When it comes to remorse, we are all prepared to say we know it when we see it, but it is so difficult to articulate what that knowledge is.'

'It is assessed by the evidence.'

'What's the evidence?' I asked.

'Your remorse.'

*

I was doing what in research circles gets called 'ethnography'. It is a science, and an art. Ethnographers conduct interviews and 'participant observation', researching and writing about groups of people by spending time with them in their environments. They record what people say, what they do and how they work, describing their practices and viewpoints. They build knowledge about cultural groups and institutions, and about people's personal, existential experience.

If you are doing ethnography, it helps to be an interloper. Anthropologists know that researching a community's local behaviour and local thought paradoxically requires some distance. It helps to be at a remove from the 'usual', not yet blind to the everyday, and therefore more able to reveal certain structures and particulars of human existence. If a person is researching remorse in the criminal justice system, say, she is perhaps better off without a law background because sometimes the most elementary questions yield the richest research data.

I continued to read legal scholarship, and to attend sentencing hearings, slowly attuning myself to the arcane language of the courts. Throughout each proceeding, as lawyers faced off with the judge and with one another about the details of the sentence and whether the offender was remorseful, the person in the dock would remain silent and lump-ish. I spoke with a forensic psychologist who told me that defence lawyers shouldn't place their clients in the witness box and have them speak, because the lawyers can't control the cross-examination. 'If you have any doubts whatsoever about the reliability or capacity of the offender to do a good showing,' he said, 'it would be just plain irresponsible to expose him to the chance he will say something stupid or really put himself in the poo.' I pictured a tightrope suspended across a swamp of shit, on which teetered a stranded offender.

Like all scientists, ethnographers are asked about their objectivity. How can their study be *objective* if it is based on *subjective* observations? In defence, a researcher cites philosopher Donna Haraway who argues that 'objectivity' is impossible to achieve: objectivity is 'a conquering gaze from nowhere', 'an illusion, a god trick', for no researcher can ever be set above and apart from the object of inquiry. Instead, so the philosopher says, we must continue to strive to produce faithful accounts of things while at the same time acknowledging and making explicit our perspective and positioning in the world.

An ethnographer is urged to consider *who and what* is this person doing the research. I listed certain of my demographic features that had helped to form the sensibility I was bringing to my study. I was a 36-year-old woman, married, mother to a healthy child. I was a second-generation European-Australian, the daughter of an Italian-Sicilian mother whose family was working-class Catholic, and of a Protestant Austrian father about whom I knew little, despite his always being around; I'd had educational opportunities, having gone to a state selective high school and to university, and I was now working in academia, a stimulating profession. I had lived, and was living, a life of privilege.

A version of this was detailed in the 55-page ethics application I had written for my university's Human Research Ethics Committee, obtaining permission to interview and observe people in the justice system.

I didn't write in the application that our lives unfold in the mysterious space between ourselves and other people; nor that an ethnographer unknowingly reveals this in the questions she asks, and in the things she notices and those she disregards. In the application I didn't mention that the etymology of 'record' is 're-' (restore), 'cordis': 'to bring back to the heart'.

*

When I was nine, I conducted a science experiment. It was a homework project for fourth grade. Our teacher had set us the task, telling us that science was all around us if we would only take the trouble to notice it. We had just trooped back to our desks after an outdoor biology lesson during which we'd been directed to notice the fibrous casings of the paperbark trees on the school oval. The bark was coming away from the towering trunks in dry, deformed pieces. I wanted to tear them right off and touch the skin underneath.

Experiments involved astute observation, our teacher explained. Watching and listening. Gathering evidence. She wrote the word 'hypothesis' on the blackboard and spoke of scientific repeatability, and I sensed how meaningful patterns could spring from disorder.

Over dinner, I relayed the assignment instructions to my parents. Family meal times were occasions to be near my father and study him. He had a strong jaw and a hawkish gaze, and, when he spoke, his satiny Viennese accent softened 'g's and 'w's. People said he was handsome like the actor Christopher Plummer. He was aloof, too, which was a quality confusing to a child, for it defied materiality: how could a person be physically present and yet so absent? At the table, he sat a child's arm length away, which meant I could watch his face and skim his hand when he reached for the butter. I tried to divine what he was thinking and feeling, and why this might be so. They say that children start doing this from a very young age: they create narratives to account for other people's reasons for action. I kept expecting him to start talking, offering up a story about himself, but he never did. I am only now, decades later, figuring out what made him who he was, and is.

My announcement at dinner about the science homework produced the intended effect: Dad's eyes brightened.

That weekend he took me to his laboratory at the university where he worked. I had been there before when I was very small; had sprawled out on the floor and drawn crayon pictures at his feet while he analysed the week's experiments for his doctoral thesis; had accompanied him and my younger sister as we went rabbit spotting in the woods on the edge of campus, following droppings and spying bunny ears disappearing into scrub. Once, I opened the fridge in his lab and found a partly dissected frog carcass resting on a Petri dish, its bloodless body bleached of life. Dad explained to me that he studied muscles and that this creature had not died in pain. His cardiac research investigated the relationship between the biochemical and mechanical properties of rat, rabbit and porcine hearts, and he was coopted to a national research centre for cardiac technology at Sydney's Royal North Shore Hospital, focusing on how a compromised heart could be assisted. I sometimes wondered if he was driven to test the limits of people's resilience, finding the precise point where organic matter ends and the spirit begins.

At the lab that Saturday when I was nine I had with me plastic sandwich bags containing samples of people's head hair. I had collected strands from half a dozen of my classmates, including from an outgoing Chinese girl; from an earnest redhead; and from my blonde best friend, who was witty and had one of those naturally amplified voices. I had strands of my sister's jet-black hair and from my brother who, even at age three, had lustrous hair you could run your hands through. I'd also plucked threads from my own wavy hair.

The aim of my project was to find out the relationship between the thickness and strength of a person's hair. In Dad's lab was a powerful microscope. We placed a strand on the glass, and I pressed my face to the viewfinder, adjusting the side knob for focus. Magnified by one hundred, the hair looked like a dissected worm made straight by the shock of death.

Attached to the microscope was a Polaroid camera that allowed us to take photos of the exaggerated wisps. We lined up the pictures and measured every strand's thickness, recording our findings in a notebook. The next step involved tethering each hair fibre to a tiny contraption we'd built that had a two-centimetre-long spring. We observed how many turns of the screw the hair could withstand before it snapped. As Dad fiddled with the spring, I rested my hand on his shoulder, soothed by the scent of his aftershave.

Back home, I stuck the Polaroid photos on a bulky piece of cardboard, and inserted the project title: 'Let's Compare Hair!'

As I wrote up the experiment, I understood how you could ask a question about the world and then design a research method whereby you might seek to answer it. And I learnt that, when it comes to studying things as they are, you should prepare to be surprised. My best friend's hair, appearing limp to the naked eye, was, when viewed as individual threads, thick and strong. And, despite the splendid appearance of my hair, the actual strands were the finest and weakest of everyone's.

I have my father's hair. I used to think it was the only thing I had inherited from him, as if the rest of him and everyone and everything that went before him were unconnected to me. I liked to think it was my mother I took after, that I had her looks and her immense capacity to love. But if fatalists are at least partly right, that we are playthings of our history and our genes, then we don't get to choose how we are shaped or what does the shaping. Then suddenly you must account for who you are and what is happening, and you're at a loss as to where to begin.

That is when you turn to the evidence, to moments from your recent and remote past, some of them memories that aren't yours:

The feel of wool underfoot in the hallway of my parents' house.

My crumple-faced baby newly beyond my skin.

A misshapen marriage proposal on an ocean headland.

The stench of ammonia and soldiers' sweat on a farm in Austria.

A mother's murmured breathing as water pools at her feet.

4

David and I met in Newtown at a café where the prongs of King Street and Enmore Road diverge, and we ordered tea that was delivered to us in a single pot, which we left to brew. He was a journalist from Melbourne. He had introduced himself to me the previous week at a law symposium at which I'd presented a paper discussing the legal literature on contrition and the fieldwork I'd just commenced. 'I once had to go before a judge,' he'd told me. 'Remorse played a big part. If you ever want to interview me, I can talk under wet cement.'

As he filled me in on the book he was writing, I regarded him. He was handsome, in his sixties and had the sort of fine features and punchy oratory that once would have cast him as a beatnik poet. I placed the voice recorder on the table between us and switched it on.

He was in court thirty years ago, he told me, because he had been charged with possession and supply of heroin. He was living in Randwick, and at ten o'clock one morning police raided his house. They found a set of scales next to his bed. He was arrested.

David pleaded guilty at Waverley Court House before an 'arsehole suburban magistrate'. He thought that for a gram and a half of smack ('chicken feed') he would get off on his middle-class credentials, that he'd get a good behaviour bond. Instead he was sentenced to six months' jail, starting now. He had received a negative report from the probation and parole guy. Before court, the guy had asked him, 'You're not still using?' David had replied: 'Look, this is the way it works. Among my cohorts, I'm the one with the drugs. But that supply would have eventually dried up. It always does. Then I wouldn't be the person with the drugs anymore. It would be somebody else in the group – somebody would have known somebody. A new little cluster would form around whatever supply line that was there. Then the very same people who'd been buying it from me, I'd be buying it from them. That's the way it happens.'

It had been a mistake to tell the probation guy this, for the man got up in court and said: 'David has no remorse for selling drugs. He continues to live in a rundown flat. He hasn't got a job, and his idea is that if he didn't sell the heroin, somebody else would. There is no remorse here.' The magistrate announced: 'I have no choice but to sentence you to a custodial sentence.' David had dope in his pocket. He was expecting to leave. As he was led out and about to be taken to Long Bay jail, he said, 'I've got to appeal! I need to appeal against this right now!' The magistrate granted him bail pending the appeal.

David was really ill. He had hepatitis B, he weighed fifty kilos, and when he collected his daughter from school, people would shuffle their children away from him. So he went into rehab, a Narcotics Anonymous–type thing for people who had found themselves bereft – morally, physically, financially. For his upcoming court appearance, he sensed that the situation was asking him for a hand-on-the-heart declaration that his life was all different, some sweeping emotional display. But the NA program he was doing was predicated on an honesty that included not pretending to feel a nobility you're not feeling. No, he wasn't using drugs; in NA, though, people don't take pledges, they don't swear off alcohol or dope. They say to themselves, *It's just today I'm not taking stuff*. It's existential. David couldn't make promises for next week. In court he couldn't say, 'It's behind me.' Instead, his lawyer told him to write a statement for the court. So he did. It was the first bit of writing he had ever done.

On the day of the appeal hearing, David's written statement was handed up to the judge and the prosecution. There was a ten-minute silence. David could see Judge Solomon was impressed. It was 'a bit of psychobabble', but the line David ran was:

> Looking at all this now, I've always been emotionally independent. When I started using drugs I thought it was just a choice, a hedonistic thing and a matter of my own sovereignty. But now, in response to it being put to me by people in the therapeutic community, I realise that cannot be right because normal people don't end up with smack habits and nearly dead.

He wrote that maybe something else was wrong with him that he'd never acknowledged: 'My mother died when I was young and I closed off for a bit. I was the kind of kid who was the least problem. But then my marriage broke up and I found myself using.' He wrote that he didn't want to be in that state anymore, that he had been free of drugs and alcohol for eight weeks, that he'd been going to NA meetings and that he was taking one day at a time. It was a story of rehabilitation, but not remorse.

After Judge Solomon read it, he looked at David, *really* looked at him. David thought, *Gotcha*. He even got the prosecutor. Then Solomon asked him about his remorse. David knew it was the deal-breaker question.

'Selling drugs. How do you feel about that now?' the judge asked.

David was stuck. He couldn't pretend to a shame he didn't feel. Six weeks out of using, it still felt normal: where people wake up in the morning and spend their day working out how to score. In court he couldn't say, 'What I did was *terrible*, such a *terrible thing*.' Then again, there was being honest, and there was being stupid.

So he tweaked it. He was on the verge of saying, 'Well I regret it.' Instead, he lowered his head and said, 'Deep regret.' He 'bullshitted a little bit' because his regret wasn't deep. Was it a performance? He didn't think of it that way. But he knew that, in an answer, fewer syllables were better. 'Deep regret' was three syllables. Best to keep it simple.

Judge Solomon nodded and turned to the prosecutor: 'I am inclined to put him on recognisance and not uphold the jail sentence. What do you think?' The prosecutor agreed, and David's jail sentence was overturned. He was given a three-year good behaviour bond.

'Kate, you are wanting to interview judges, yes?' David asked me. 'If you ever speak with Judge Solomon, send him my regards. Tell him I've been clean for thirty years. Tell him it turned out alright. You know, I think remorse is an old person's game. It took me years to really regret selling heroin, and the regret mainly has to do with my family. My wife and I reconciled. We are still together. But even now I worry about my daughter. I still have a lot of remorse. What pains me most is that she got that protective thing kids get. She worried about me all the time. Someone told her, "Your dad's gonna die." Kids take it on in some way. They feel responsible. So, anyway, as I said, remorse is an old person's game. The time it takes to align your personal view with a larger societal view – to align yourself with a larger consciousness – is really slow. For this reason I don't think it is possible for a person, especially a young person, to experience true remorse between the time they have committed an offence and the time they front up to the court hearing.'

*

There are photos of my father holding me as a newborn, and then as a toddler in our backyard among piles of leaves. I look at them and feel the warmth of his chest and the crunch of the autumn ground.

It is easy to love a baby, its animal need for care. But as children grow more human-like, they become unwelcome mirrors for their parents.

For three decades, Dad did not demonstrate a lot of fondness towards my siblings and me. We felt we gave him little joy. He seemed the object of a fairy-tale curse, and whenever he was around, a greyness descended on our household. For reasons I am still coming to understand, this curse lifted several years ago when he was in his mid-sixties; his deep love for my sister, my brother and me, and for our young families, has ever after been a strong, steady glow. We revel in this paternal devotion. During my first thirty years, however, there were few expressions of affection from him. I can count them, they are easily tallied for their conspicuousness, and when I string them together, an accidentally tender portrait emerges.

Ethnographers are familiar with this pitfall: how a few anecdotes placed side by side can inadvertently create an untruth. It is the persistent problem of 'event' versus 'background'. To identify and reflect on the former, about happenings with beginnings, middles and ends, feels natural, straightforward. It is a practice the justice system executes with flair: forensically reconstructing a delimited occurrence or occurrences. But mostly we live our lives in the latter, in background: the unmarked, the anodyne, the uneventful. This shadow-living works on us stealthily. When attempting to write of it, one must somehow conjure an entire backdrop, a reality built from the accumulation of thousands of tiny repeated experiences. Grammatically speaking, then, a writer finds herself shifting into the habitual past, enlisting the aid of 'would' and 'used to'.

On weekends my father would compile lists of chores and attend to each one robotically. I would watch him mowing the lawn or fixing a door jamb, and I'd search for signs of animation. His blankness was cause for agitation for it felt empty, un-person-like. Sometimes I'd try to coax him back into his body: I would find him in the burgundy armchair reading books about Ancient Greek battles and mighty gods, and I'd lean in to kiss his cheek. But he'd flinch, irritated, and would retreat to the bedroom and close the door, or he'd drive to his laboratory to work. I was at a friend's house once when I was ten and watched the way her father squeezed her to him, ruffling her hair, the two of them laughing and joking. The intimacy of the scene struck me as strange and tremendous, for all I knew was a father who turned his eyes and ears away from his children. I wished Dad would leave our family and never return so that I might replace his cheerless presence with an imagined father. I could daydream into existence a sunny man.

My mother saw what was happening at home and tried to make up for it. She figured she could love us twice as hard, and ran herself ragged in her enactments of care. She would shop, cook, bake and clean; sew and mend our clothes; help us with schoolwork; and drive us to activities; all the while holding down her twin jobs as a freelance health journalist and a part-time high-school maths teacher. Most Sundays she would take us to her parents' house where we would have Italian lunches with our grandparents and Mum's six younger brothers. The abundant affection my sister, brother and I received from our mother and her kin further exposed the chasm between our father and us kids. I sensed this brokenness, believed myself responsible and stubbornly tried to mend it. But any effort to seek out Dad to share something of myself only annoyed him – 'What *is* it?' he'd snap before shooing me away.

To be noticed by our father either meant you were injured, or you were being blamed for something. Dad was good in a crisis ('good in a crisis' being the sort of label that gets attached to people for whom ordinary communal exchange is a challenge), and he would act swiftly to alleviate his children's illnesses and broken bones. In the absence of crises, we were left with reproof. He would see that his stapler was missing from its usual spot ('Who had it last?'), or that the bathroom tap was not turned off quite properly ('It's dripping!'), or had been turned off with too much force ('You'll damage the washer!'), and would come looking for the guilty party. Fathers can be frightening figures, their height and weight, their bellow. Ours did not hit us, although we kept expecting him to. We never felt safe. His explosions were unpredictable, the sudden mutation from coolness to heat, and the result was that my material reality of space, time and event grew distorted. I learnt to see myself as a chronic wrongdoer even when I wasn't. And there was no pardon either. If, after a transgression, or perceived transgression, I approached Dad and whispered, 'Sorry', there were pursed lips and stoniness. The consequence of even the smallest error was exile.

No parent can possibly comprehend the full impact they have, quite how much they matter. My father could not see that his behaviour was shaping our universe because, when it came to relationships, he believed he was inconsequential. Worse: he *yearned* to be inconsequential. Our mother knew something of his history and that her husband's darkness masked his struggle to participate in intimate family life, as well as self-loathing to do with long-ago events for which he had no business being sorry.

As my father brooded and raged about ghosts, he was crippling the possibility of being close to his children, because children never forget. They grow up and move out, brushing aside those early years, for nothing exceptional happened when they were little: no single flagrant incident occurred around which to coalesce this persistent ache of theirs. But then eventually those children have their own babies, and, without realising they are doing it, they return to their childhood home. This returning is so instinctive, so collaborative, that, linguistically, subjects and objects jumble themselves. The childhood home becomes the doer. The home does the returning. The home returns to you.

*

At the tip of the narrow street where my husband, our daughter and I lived was scrubland that stretched out to a sandstone outcrop and, deep below it, the ocean.

On my days off with Jemima, we would read *The Cat in the Hat* and *We're Going on a Bear Hunt*, and make houses from blocks, and artworks from cupcake patty pans and glue; and when I was due to shower or hang out the washing, I'd turn on *Play School* and let her stand there mesmerised by the dress-ups and the songs.

Then we would trundle outside and past the sixteen houses that buffered us from the edge of the world. The broad cliff ledge had pleasant rocks for sitting and jumping. Padded out in her lolly-pink jacket, her nappy and toddler chub, Jemima would scramble up a metre-high shelf, me gripping a fistful of her clothing like a crane as I guided her flight. Afterwards we'd putter down the snaking path to the shops for bread for lunch, before retracing our steps home. In the afternoons I'd lie with her on the double bed, hoping she would sleep, knowing she wouldn't. Sometimes a rivulet of sunlight would spill into the bedroom. It illuminated the air, revealing a secret solar system of dust particles floating in their own miniature orbits.

In the months after Jemima was born, when my working life had retreated, I decelerated to such a point that the passing of time felt glacial. I was using my unfamiliar body in alien ways, sitting breastfeeding on and off for hours, day and night, and drifting between the kitchen, the washing machine and the bedroom. The lobotomy-like tiredness meant I couldn't read, although I wanted badly to, and instead I watched a lot of television. The trillions of synapses in my brain were so sluggish that I felt unable to make basic decisions. One afternoon a shop assistant found me in a supermarket aisle, Jemima strapped to my chest, staring at columns of loo paper, incapable of choosing which pack to buy. He said I had been standing there for fifteen minutes.

This sense of slowness was confused by an altogether different recognition: how rapidly my baby was developing. More than once I would recover a jumpsuit from the washing line, the item having fit Jemima the day before, only to discover that, like a physics miracle, her newly filled-out legs and torso had outgrown it. Meanwhile my own development felt retarded. It was as if together she and I made up velocity's extremes.

Before Jemima, I was a quick, forward-moving thing. I was so reliant on momentum, as if adrenaline was life itself, that relaxation unnerved me. I never took a holiday for longer than a week, didn't take a 'year off' as my friends did to go backpacking overseas, and instead sped virtually uninterrupted from undergraduate degree to PhD to occupation. Hurried motion, I now realise, enabled me to suspend the loop of error I had grown up imagining myself in. I could keep the past at bay. The faster I moved, the less aware I was *of* time in any expansive sense. When you are racing, it is all about the next five minutes, and the five minutes after that. It's a repudiation of cause and effect.

At home with the baby, however, my experience of life's tempo changed from that of a mayfly to one of a geologist, as I was thrust into what felt like a never-ending stasis that I had previously only ever associated with the seriously ill. The hours, days and years I'd left behind surged upon me and I could do nothing but let them yank me about, leaving me broken and sore. Remorse depends on time for its existence. Without time, there is no consequence. When I was nineteen, my mother's mother – a woman with a social-work degree, who raised seven children, who worked as Australia's first agony aunt for a national magazine, who routinely baked meals for her Italian family of twenty, and who rarely, if ever, sat still – had a massive stroke that left her wheelchair-bound. She was sixty-seven. To me the horror of it was her inertness and the awareness of time it brought with it. While her mind still functioned, her left arm was all but paralysed and she was practically frozen from the waist down. In the final two decades of her life, her days and nights were spent reflecting. *Reflectere*: to bend back. I shuddered at the prospect of being unable to outrun my own history.

Stationed on the sofa breastfeeding, I would gaze at Jemima's velvety face and tiny hands as they clasped my pinky. *How privileged I am to be your mother*, I'd think with thick gratitude, but would then be flooded by self-doubt and admonishment regarding everything I'd ever done and every future decision I would make, for motherhood supplies continual opportunities to fail. As my milk poured into my baby, I imagined her as a creature outside time, forever free from a past and therefore free from blame. I would immediately catch myself (*such pressure to place on those tiny shoulders!*), and instead would pray she might simply be 'good'. Then I'd wonder what 'good' even meant.

Some philosophers say that to feel remorse for a minor wrong you have committed is to be neurotic, and that 'compunction' is the better term. The category of 'remorse', they say, should be preserved for grave misdeeds. But what happens when your small wrongs, and a few medium-sized ones, come upon you in one great gush? They roll into one another, and you are unable to discern what order of regret you should attach to each thing, nor if reconciliation is possible. When I was seven, I said that a kind, quiet girl in my class was 'fat'; when I was eight, I stole a pair of scissors from my classmate who owned Japanese stationery; when I was eleven, I was mean to my sister on our way to a dress-up party, me as Minnie Mouse, her as Olive Oyl; when I was thirteen, I nagged Mum and she distractedly brought her hand down on an erect paring knife; when I was fourteen, I took money that wasn't mine; when I was sixteen, I distressed my parents by disappearing for two days with a guy much older than me; when I was nineteen, I treated a friend with contempt; and when I was twenty-one, I slept with someone else's boyfriend. I could go on.

I was christened Catholic but wasn't raised as one, and have never been to confession. I suspect that the excursion would be hobbled by my inability to understand the relationship between atonement and time. You sit in the confession booth and relay your sins; the priest metes out your penance. Is it in the reciting of the Hail Marys that the sin is forgiven? Are you free of it then? What if, in the meantime, you have sinned again? Are you always in arrears? Despite this puzzle, it now occurs to me that growing up I might have benefited from confession if for no other reason than it enforces stillness and frank contemplation. I might have done what David said must be done, which is to align myself with a larger consciousness. It would have meant dealing with slip-ups one at a time, as they occurred, rather than racing onwards, leaving them to pile up in my wake.

In the same year as my grandmother's stroke, I became friends with a guy in my philosophy class at uni. He was unlike us other teenagers in that his parents had recently died and therefore he had adopted a disconcerting self-sufficiency that was further augmented by virtue of his being extremely bright. Dux of his posh private boys' school, he was excelling in philosophy and goodness knows what else, while the rest of us wrestled with 'Intermediate Logic' and 'Philosophy of Mind'. We would hang out often, for talk came easily to us. We also did indoor rock-climbing together. I must have really liked him because it didn't come naturally to me. Climbing required patience, balance and repetition, not the speed and uni-direction I was used to in my other sports. We took turns belaying. I stood below and watched him ascend. He had no fear of falling. Grasping a bright orange foothold and hoisting himself up, flattening his torso to the wall, sometimes he would slip, or he'd miss the protrusion entirely, and would drop suddenly away. Instead of clinging to the rope, eyes closed, as I would have done, begging to be inched down to safety, he'd remain swinging up there, like a *deus ex machina* in a Greek play, examining the upwards path and assessing where he'd erred. Then he'd go again and again until he reached the top.

It was his poise – no, his *pause* – that was so enthralling. He would pause just long enough for his immediate past, those previous few minutes, to rush towards and into him so that he might learn from his own wrong-footedness.

5

Days after speaking with David I arrived at the Supreme Court for the sentencing of the woman who had killed the 21-year-old with her car. Onlookers gathered in the foyer and unacknowledged electricity hummed among us.

The woman's mother stood rigidly at the entrance of the courtroom, clutching the *Daily Telegraph*, the front-page headline: 'No One Will Pay'. It wasn't her daughter the paper referred to. A day earlier, the manslaughter charge against Mark Wilhelm, the man thought to be responsible for Dianne Brimble's death on a cruise ship, had been dropped.

I sat on a wooden bench under the dramatic staircase. An elderly man sat at the other end. Nodding at my notebook, he smiled and told me he was a retiree who routinely visited the courts because he liked 'seeing the justice system in action'. As we filed inside, I asked him if he thought that the woman was remorseful.

'She has seemed very down,' he said. 'But it is hard to say whether it's for herself or for what she has done. The judge will be able to tell.'

'How?' I asked.

'He has had so much experience. He knows character.'

We found seats near the back. The victim's parents sat at the centre, the father producing from his bag an A4-sized photo of his dead son and gently placing it on the bench between him and his wife.

The offender emerged from her staircase, looked over to find her mother, and sat alone in the dock with two guards close by.

'All rise!' We stood. The judge entered, seated himself, and launched into reading aloud the printed-out pages that lay before him: 'The offender was convicted by a jury of murder arising from an incident during which she intentionally drove a motor vehicle at the deceased . . .'

Having never before attended a sentencing, I didn't know how long it might take. I wondered if it would be over in less than a minute, the judge announcing the conviction followed by the number of years the offender was to spend in prison. But the judgment took the judge half an hour to read out.

We listened as His Honour presented a plot-driven narrative laden with verbs I would come to recognise as typical of court judgments. The story of the night of the victim's death began in pluperfect tense, the effect being one of impending tragedy: 'The deceased, his brother [. . .], and a number of other young persons had gathered at [the brother's] home principally to record music [. . .] In the meantime the offender had left her premises with a companion to purchase cigarettes at a convenience store.'

As the account drew closer to the killing, it switched to simple past tense and ballooned out with distressing detail: 'The offender drove along Lithgow Street and suddenly turned into one of the driveways at the very moment that the deceased was walking across the driveway. She either struck him or came very close to him and he avoided the vehicle at the last moment.' We heard how the deceased remonstrated with the car's occupants, before being pulled away by one of his friends; how he waited behind an industrial bin on the curb; how he got to his feet; how he came out from behind the bins to cross a driveway; how the headlights of the offender's vehicle appeared to switch to high beam; how the vehicle drove diagonally from the street, mounting the curb; how the car made contact with the deceased who was struck by the front of the vehicle and carried forward; and how the 'vehicle continued until it careered down a flight of stairs to a gym at the corner of the building, taking the deceased with it and crushing him beneath the vehicle at the foot of the stairs'.

Occasionally the judge inserted himself as an authoritative interpreter ('It seems obvious to me . . .'; 'I believe that . . .'; 'I have no doubt that . . .'), but the state of mind about which His Honour was most concerned was that of the woman. We heard how, after striking the young man, she tried to put the car in reverse but it did not move; how the deceased's brother and friends came rushing over and tried to lift the vehicle off the young man, and how the woman tried to help; and how she was in 'a very distressed state and concerned that she may have killed the deceased'.

What followed were a number of casually dropped bombshells. We learnt that ten years ago the woman had attacked her unsuspecting husband with a kitchen knife. They'd had an argument. He was lying facedown on the lounge when she approached him and stabbed him twice. She was convicted of 'malicious wounding'. We learnt that eight years ago she had illegally entered the house of a woman who she claimed owed her money. She climbed through a window and began punching the victim. She was convicted of 'assault occasioning actual bodily harm'. Listening to this, I wondered if there had been an irresponsible oversight on the part of the courts that this information had not been made public earlier. And yet I had to remind myself that this is precisely why the information was kept concealed. A person's guilt is judged on the facts of the case, not on her past. Her criminal history becomes relevant only during sentencing.

The judge summed up the woman's life in a single sad paragraph: she was born in 1971, psychiatric problems first became evident in her school years and she started using alcohol and cannabis, she left school at fifteen, she was diagnosed as having Attention Deficit Hyperactivity Disorder at twenty, at age twenty-one she started using heroin, she was diagnosed with depression and the depression increased after she was sexually assaulted at the age of thirty, and she was the mother of a fourteen-year-old boy.

His Honour turned to the woman's feelings: 'I accept that she was immediately remorseful [. . .] Her remorse is confirmed by the letter from the chaplain at the prison. There is also considerable evidence of her remorse in the psychological notes from the Department of Corrective Services.'

Then came the moment. The judge asked the offender to stand. The woman in the dock rose and stiffly turned to the front.

'The offender is sentenced to a term of imprisonment made up of a non-parole period of eighteen years and nine months and a balance term of six years and three months [. . .] This is in effect a sentence of imprisonment for twenty-five years.'

His Honour stood, we stood and he exited. My elderly companion whispered to me: 'We have excellent judges. They get things right ninety-five per cent of the time.'

The woman looked emotionless. Her mother went to her.

The audience heaved towards the door as the boy's parents crumpled back into their seats.

After the woman had been led back down the staircase and bundled into a car that would deliver her to prison, the young man's parents, dazed, finally stepped outside to the loitering news crews. A bouquet of microphones was held out towards them. The father read from a bit of paper he held in both hands.

'The woman who murdered our son has been sentenced to twenty-five years in prison,' he said. 'We have been sentenced to a lifetime of anguish.'

Asked about the offender's remorse, the mother replied: 'We have seen no sign of contrition in her.'

They turned from the throng and carried themselves away up the road.

Stunned, I remained in the middle of the footpath, unable to harmonise the judge's jargon with the woman's wrecked life and the parents' absolute despair. Eventually I made myself start walking. On Macquarie Street I passed evenly bedded-out London plane trees and edifices of civil society – the Mint, Sydney Hospital, Parliament House, the State Library – all the while concentrating on the splodges of sunlight under my feet.

How had His Honour arrived at the woman's sentence? What precisely had convinced him of her remorse? He'd used something called a 'stepped approach'. There were 'different categories of murder'. He'd had to consider the 'objective seriousness of the offence'. He spoke of 'aggravating' and 'mitigating' factors, and of the 'statutory ratio between the non-parole period and the total term'. He'd announced it was a murder of a mid-level range, being neither planned nor wholly spontaneous. And he had reduced the standard non-parole period from twenty years to eighteen years and nine months because of the woman's 'immediate and continuing remorse'.

At Circular Quay, I took in the twinkling harbour and the fat, rude honks of the ferries.

I knew that judges assess crimes in relation to the law. But they must also sit opposite people and decide who they are and what to do with them.

His Honour had sat opposite the woman. He'd read reports from a forensic psychologist and from a prison chaplain. He had concluded that her repentance was sincere. And yet the boy's parents didn't accept it.

*

I used to walk down the street imagining myself as having the dimensions of paper. By that I mean flat. I passed strangers at bus stops and envisioned myself as a crisp, blank A4 sheet.

This was fifteen years ago when I was reading anthropology and discovering the different shapes of people: the Warlpiri people in northern Australia who coalesce person and country, fusing the body and the environment in terms of internal physiology so that a sacred site, for instance, is a womb; the Yolmo Sherpa community in Nepal for whom a sudden fright causes a person's soul to vacate their body and wander about the countryside, a shaman divining how their soul was lost, where it has wandered and how best to retrieve it.

I read about these different shapes and I wondered if I could change mine. Picturing myself flat was an experiment in depthlessness, interrupting my customary self-experience: that is, a being with a dark, hidden interior and a fleshy exterior. Through this imagining I was trying to shake off at least two thousand years of western thinking: the radical new Christian World in which people were defined by their inner desires and intentions, through to modern psychology where the human being has a rational, conscious mind consumed by subconscious, irrational impulses. In other words, I was trying to shake off the West's topography of a person as a self-examining, confessing creature.

When I was a piece of paper, I felt peaceful. My mind stopped whirring because, in these new terms, such secret whirring would be read on the public page; or, better still, there was simply no easy spot (no brain, no physical matter) within which the whirring could take place. But I could never remain paper for long. Within seconds I had spontaneous ponderings. And it was no use conceiving of anyone around me as paper, either, because I was too curious about people's roiling thoughts and feelings.

During court hearings I noticed the ordinary presence of armfuls of paper, stapled pages authoritatively giving shape to the offender.

They were reports written by forensic psychiatrists and psychologists detailing people's inner chaos. Such documents not only spat out offenders' ghastly personal histories in the manner of compressed obituaries; they also sketched out what sort of person they were, what they were like, and sometimes they even proclaimed that the offender was contrite. How this was assessed I didn't know.

The judge had referred to a psychological report when he'd sentenced that woman. A clinician had narrated for the court what the offender really thought and felt, who she really was, and that evaluation had been used to assist His Honour in determining her remorse. The report had not been made public. I wondered what it contained.

I emailed the judge. I said that I was an academic and a writer, that I had commenced research on the role of remorse in the justice system, and I asked if His Honour would be prepared to meet with me.

In the meantime, I visited a forensic psychiatrist. His dim-lit office had the feel of a nineteenth-century library. There was no leather couch. There was, however, a smart leather chair. As I sat I felt the warmth of its seat. The room smelt sweet, pheromones secreted by the client who'd just left and whom I hadn't seen as I waited in a separate little area. The psychiatrist was in his fifties and looked like an actor playing a physician; reminiscent of Charlie Chaplin, he didn't quite manage to fill the dark suit he was wearing.

'Remorse is in the eye of the beholder,' he told me. 'There is no objective way of measuring it. It's not a psychiatric symptom. Any psychiatrist or psychologist who offers his opinion as to a person's remorse is, in my view, working outside his brief.'

He said that, when he used to write pre-sentence reports, defence lawyers pressured him to testify to their client's remorse: 'Courtrooms are lawyers' territory and if you go in as a naïve witness who has never done this before, you are totally bamboozled and overwhelmed by a very frightening experience.'

I wondered about the numbers of psychiatrists and psychologists writing court reports on people's remorse, and I wondered how many of them were bamboozled.

'There are infinite layers of meaning in what people tell you,' he said. 'Just because offenders tell you they feel remorseful means nothing more than they tell you they feel remorseful. They can *weep* and tell you that they feel remorse, but, again, the *meaning* of that is a different question.'

Not only did he believe that remorse was untestable, he never encountered it in his patients: 'If somebody is sad and melancholic – that intense hopelessness – and is feeling they are a worthless individual and that they have done a terrible thing and that they should be punished and that they are the source of all suffering in the world, I would consider this a pathological symptom of a severe depressive condition. This feeling that they have may, in fact, not represent a realistic appraisal of their own remorse. It's more the feeling of exaggerated negativity that comes from an illness.'

Of course, he did believe there was such a thing as remorse. It's just that his patients didn't present with it. Then again, he didn't exactly go looking for it. When seeing inmates, the most common thing people told him was simply: 'I didn't *do* it, Doc.'

According to him, questions of remorse are best left to the lawyers.

'It is a matter of legal argument,' he said finally. 'As a doctor, I'm there to provide medical care for these people. I'm not there to weigh up moral issues. That's for the judge to do.'

Days later I phoned a forensic psychologist who wrote the very court reports about which the psychiatrist was scathing. 'The psychiatrist you spoke with was in a shitty mood,' he bristled. 'Yes, remorse is untestable. Lots of things are untestable. The whole role of being an expert in human behaviour is that you are constructing an understanding of somebody. You're not testing it. To explore remorse you need to explore it idiosyncratically: the specifics of the offence, and the specifics of the people who are affected by the offence.'

What confounded me about the idea of spilling your remorse to a doctor who in turn spills it to the court is that surely being sorry is the sort of thing that shouldn't be shared with a clinician but with the person you have wronged.

When I was in my early twenties I saw a counsellor a few times. My boyfriend and I had lived together for a couple of years, and we had recently separated. I was heartbroken. I had left full-time work, had meekly re-entered university study, and I felt directionless, or rather anchorless, as, paradoxically, for me, an anchor enables meaningful motion.

The counsellor was a well-meaning woman with pasty make-up and viciously blow-dried hair. I had betrayed my boyfriend. It was a brief affair with a work colleague. I was riddled with guilt. I wanted to confess to him. 'Don't,' she said. She questioned my motives: 'Are you just trying to unburden yourself? What would be achieved by speaking with him?' She told me to write the apology and then burn it.

At home, I scribbled down my shame on a crisp A4 sheet. On the concrete landing outside my apartment I lit a match and watched the paper ignite and dissolve into carbon scraps that were carried skywards. I felt off the hook: it was pardon without confrontation. But I also had the nagging sense that I was cheating. Here I was asking for absolution, not from the person whom I'd injured, but from the unseen wind.

6

My husband was moody. The flow of his freelance work had reduced to a trickle, and he had become cool and withdrawn at home. I felt wounded by the distance between us, a space so palpable that it had its own forlorn shape. Occasionally Brad would mumble something about retraining, but his heart wasn't in it, not enough to desert what he knew and loved. Instead he existed in a sort of stasis.

He was with Jemima on Wednesdays and Fridays while I was at work. He took her to Taronga Zoo to see the meerkats, or to the playground with the king-sized climbing frame, or to Sydney Airport where they stationed themselves at the fence near the runways and watched the planes take off and land. A childish part of me was envious of their adventures, jealous of my baby daughter's relationship with her father, his easy affection towards her. They would burst in, sweaty and satisfied with their outing, and, while she'd gallop over to greet me with cuddles and thousands of kisses, Brad would hold back. He'd say nothing as he made himself a coffee, disappearing into the study to chip away at a film treatment.

The job of parenthood is hard no matter the circumstances, and is uniquely hard on people prone to introspection. For much of our marriage, we had spent our mornings – sometimes entire days – in happy silence, united in our practice of reading, thinking, reflecting, creating. Brad was a director, mainly of television commercials, but was also developing drama projects. I had begun publishing nonfiction, and was longing to write more. Before our baby arrived, when it was just the two of us, we went for walks along the coast, sharing ideas, nurturing dreams of the beautiful, important works we would make.

Now, though, we saw in ourselves only vanquished potential, the quick deaths and slow dying of lives that would never come to pass: what we might have done, might have achieved; who we might have become. We didn't talk about this feeling, it being painful and shamefully egoistic. Our grief was so abundant that it assumed a dense weight throughout our home, obstructing passages we might have otherwise used to reach one another.

*

I left Jemima with Brad one night and had dinner with three school friends – a novelist, a playwright and a politician – at a Lebanese restaurant in Glebe. We sat upstairs in the 'Sultan's Lounge', with geranium-red cushions and the smoky perfume of spices and flame. The politician was campaigning for the upcoming state election. She had us in hysterics as she recounted a major photo shoot she'd had that week: upon examining the head-shots of her smiling face, her publicity team tactlessly lamented the limitations of Photoshop.

They asked what I was working on. I told them about the bombastic defence lawyer, about David's performance in court, and about capital cases in the US, where juries determined both the guilt of a person and the sentence, and where a person's apparent remorse influenced the granting of mercy in death penalty decisions. I told them about the woman's case I'd observed, her murder conviction, reciting the legal phrase: 'the offender has provided evidence that he or she has accepted responsibility for his or her actions'. We agreed it would be difficult to demonstrate remorse if you had contested the charge. Remorse is a sign of guilt. If you have pleaded not guilty, and you are subsequently found guilty, how can you then show contrition? We talked of cases of wrongful conviction, like Lindy Chamberlain's. She was jailed for a murder that never occurred, and was further punished for not expressing remorse. A law scholar pointed out that, in the moral ordering of convicted offenders, where the remorseful are seemingly the most deserving of compassion, Chamberlain was ranked at the very bottom. As for the woman who had killed that young man with her car, she'd pleaded guilty to manslaughter, but not to murder. It was her car that hit him. She took some responsibility, but not total responsibility. The jury, however, found that she both *committed* a guilty act and that she *intended* to commit it; that she had *mens rea*, a guilty mind.

Together my friends and I mulled over the feeling of remorse, trying to define it. We enlisted other feelings – grief, regret – and found ourselves caught in the airy realm of emotion, so entirely embedded in private experience that it was beyond the reach of words.

There began a high-pitched drumming, a hypnotic 2/4 rhythm, and a mermaid creature appeared, with long hair, a beaded bust-piece and a swirling skirt worn low. The belly dancer positioned herself among the tables, the waiters gliding around her, and gradually her arms floated out from her body, while her abdomen, at first an organised, homogenous form, sprang to life and separated into discrete dancing parts. In the face of such focused, physical frenzy, I was pulled into a sort of meditative state. I saw that, yes, remorse is closely related to 'responsibility', 'shame' and 'guilt', but really it is a different class of thing. You can feel shame, while not feeling remorse. You can take responsibility, while feeling neither shame nor remorse. As for guilt, it is a passive, inward-directed state, whereas remorse is active and dynamic. Remorse is the outward yearning for atonement. It is suffering made visible.

That night I didn't sleep. The wine I'd had at dinner triggered erratic synaptic activity.

Is the remorse you feel always *yours*? Can it be inherited genetically, like the shape of your nose or brow, so that you and your children carry old cells from long ago?

I sensed the distant past, or it came and found me, and I felt the panic, shame and rage of a young woman whom I recognised by the scroll of her hair as my father's mother. It was surprising, not least because I'd never met my paternal grandmother, Elizabeth – she'd died two years to the day before I was born – and because I know her image only from a handful of smudgy black-and-white photographs buried in a heavy album on my parents' shelf.

But in my mind's eye I saw her watching young men in uniforms who in turn were watching her and her small son. Vienna, 1945. Allied soldiers invade Austria. My skinny-kneed father scurries along bombed city streets, watching and guessing, always guessing, what men are thinking and what they might do next.

*

Jemima and I visited my parents at their place, in the house where I grew up. Mum had cooked pasta ragu and chicken schnitzel, Jemima's favourite, and as the two of them set the table together, Dad and I discussed the university. He listened brightly as I talked about my teaching, my PhD students and my court research, and when Mum called us over to eat, he and I walked to the table, arms linked. After lunch, he led Jemima outside towards a strawberry that had reddened in the night.

When he retired from the university, around the time that curse of his lifted, my father viewed the garden with revived imagination.

For more than three decades he had attended to the backyard in a utilitarian way, mowing the lawn and monitoring tree branches for dangerous overhang. He even built from scratch a large freestanding pergola complete with landscaping, which involved moving tonnes of soil by hand. The flower beds he left to Mum and her green thumb, my mother's gardening philosophy being that of a rambling kind. Plants, she contends, should bunk in together and sprawl and stretch out wherever they please. I have always loved watching her move slowly among the tibouchinas, Cécile Brünner roses, sweet peas and lamb's ears, humming to them, some mornings coming upon a secret shoot, the fruit of seeds she's forgotten she sowed.

With new hours at home, Dad designated a portion of the yard for a vegetable project. Instead of adopting Mum's improvisatory technique, he mapped and planned. He plotted the movement of the sun, and researched soil and soil depth. He and my uncle dug and cleared a section at the back near the old pepper tree, sawing and assembling treated pine sleepers of the non-arsenic variety; they created two large stepped boxes with fertile earth, and Dad planted tomatoes, beans, lettuces, broccoli, cucumbers. He cared for the seedlings, the arrangement being that because he kept up his side of things, they should keep up theirs – which they did, and have – but he didn't count on the possums and the brush turkeys, the rabbits, snails, slugs and bandicoots that raid the produce at will. Each night he draped the veggie boxes with bridal-style netting to fend off looters.

Through the window I watched my father and my daughter crouching at the patch, and him plucking the strawberry for her. He caught my eye and smiled. A shyness crept over me. It was how I mostly felt around him nowadays: shy. He was no longer the forbidding father, and yet a lifetime of habit had left me with no capacity to approach him other than to talk about my professional life. Our relationship rested on a bedrock of complicated feeling.

It is odd to reach adulthood, and to have your own baby, and all the while be without a satisfying picture of your parent's early life. It is like having black spots in your vision. Months into the remorse project, I did not yet have the fortitude to ask Dad to shed light on those spots. I had approached the subject many times previously but had been rebuffed, and a child never grows used to a parent's displeasure. When I read that 'Viennese society is built on secrets', I gave up entirely. Almost everything I knew about him was from my mother, and from my father's sister before she died, and from reading history. I learnt what I could from studying my father too, as if his gait or the outline of his hands might tell me some small thing.

I knew that he was born in May 1943, and that three days before his second birthday, when the bells proclaimed peace and the end of war in Europe, Vienna was a shattered city. Thousands of unburied bodies lay under ruins, thousands of homes had been wholly or partially destroyed, and tens of thousands of people left homeless. There was no gas, electricity or phone, and subsistence levels had dwindled to almost nothing. For six weeks no food was delivered to the city, and half the newborn children had perished. Eventually Vienna's one-and-a-half million inhabitants relied on several dozen lorries available to bring in supplies, the Russian authorities fixing the daily rationing intake.

Most Austrians were Catholic, but Dad's family was Lutheran, not that God was much of a talking point at this time in Austria, a country preoccupied with frantically trying to forget its Nazi ties. In 1945, the Allies estimated that there were more than half a million Austrian Nazis; of the 50,000 or so judged as having actual power during the Reich and therefore incriminated, some tried to conceal their pasts, or they hid, or killed themselves. The country began performing a sort of amnesia. It made a point of celebrating its anti-German history by publishing books on Austria's resistance to Prussia during the Seven Years' War; people spoke in an Austrian dialect;

and the men wore Styrian hats and suits, and the women dirndls, to proclaim cultural difference. The Moscow Declaration of 1943 had affirmed the Allies' acceptance, officially at least, that the Austrians were Hitler's first victims, but Russian soldiers were dubious. Jeeps patrolled the streets, each jeep containing four occupants, one from each of the occupying forces (France, the United States, Soviet Union and United Kingdom) and this maintained some sort of stability, the men keeping an eye on one another, taking it in turns to drive. In the minds of the Viennese, though, there was an expressed dread of the Red Army soldier. After peace was declared, and after Vienna was carved up into four occupation zones, the Russian quarter was, for a time, lawless. Carol Reed's film *The Third Man* depicts Vienna in a sort of half-death, hills of rubble and twilight shadows, its people in a moral limbo. It was shot in 1948 when Dad was five years old. Each time I watch it I look out for a small boy running through the streets.

Now whenever I visited my parents, it wasn't that I expected Dad to orate his autobiography, or to produce a machine-gun expulsion of anecdotes. What I wanted were some of his self-defining memories. I needed from him stories of events that he believed made him who he was. Despite my willingness to intrude on the life-details of the people I was interviewing, however, I feared that such a conversation with Dad would cause titanic fissures I couldn't bear. When you grow up sensing pain in a parent, you don't ask to see the wounds; you try to heal them. You believe you can save your father from what has already happened.

7

It had been weeks since my email and I hadn't heard back from the judge. Perhaps he couldn't, or wouldn't, talk to me.

I spent entire days at Sydney's Downing Centre courts, moving from courtroom to courtroom like a stubborn ghost. The building, opposite Hyde Park, had a theatrical nostalgia about it, having been built in 1908 as a department store for Mark Foy's; from Liverpool Street it looked like a wedding cake – thick frosting with a candy lemon trim – and inside was brightly tiled mosaic flooring. The rest of the interior was utterly worn out. The upstairs carpeting was fraying, the windows were coated with grime, the chairs threadbare. Impervious to the building's history, schoolchildren on excursions were escorted into hearings to learn the law, but grew bored and picked at the honeycomb-coloured foam poking through the seats.

I was attending local court sessions, watching magistrates confront offenders. A man was fined $500 for possessing marijuana, the magistrate telling him: 'Despite what your attitude is to the use and possession of cannabis, it is still illegal.' A man was sentenced to prison for larceny and for presenting false cheques amounting to $40,000, the magistrate announcing: 'These are very serious matters.'

Galling as it was to admit, each confrontation I witnessed was feeding some basic human lust for the spectacle of denunciation. An official purpose of sentencing was just that – to publicly denounce the offence – and it reminded me of the way kids watch other kids get into trouble.

At primary school, I had shared classes with boys who flicked elastic bands, who drew rude sketches in library books, who bruised one another with tennis balls; girls who chatted too much, who put nasty notes in school mates' bags, who nicked lollies from the corner store. I was not like these kids, I was mostly a good girl, and I wondered why other children didn't *just behave themselves* and therefore avoid what was coming to them. When a boy half my size was marched to the front of the classroom and made to sit at the teacher's feet, his glum form slumped on the emerald carpet; when another boy was ordered to stand in the corner and face the wall; and when a girl was sent to the principal's office, I watched the unfolding dramas. It wasn't that I enjoyed seeing my peers punished. But I couldn't look away either. It did something to my skin, a prickly rush.

Understanding this adrenaline entailed a rethinking of the categories of 'singular' and 'plural'.

As a Year 5 class, we were an 'it', so when little Mark Reynolds wouldn't sit still and *show some respect*, and when Mr Scott strode over, seized the boy by his collar and hauled him outside, Mark was, simultaneously, both one of us, and us all. For the class, the shock was seeing one of our own singled out.

The rush comes from recognising that the disgraced child is both you and not you. We lived through Mark's humiliation – which is what Aristotle contemplated when he wrote about tragedy: how watching other people's bad luck, their follies and catastrophe, has a cathartic effect, purging us of fear and pity. (No one is certain how Aristotle saw the actual technique of catharsis working, but I thought of it as a bit like preparing eggplant: how a sprinkle of salt leaches bitterness from the flesh.)

I wondered if public hunger for stories of crime and justice was a mechanism for people's absolution; that by watching courtroom confrontation and denunciation, we might, vicariously, be rid of our own shame and remorse.

Another thing happens too.

As I saw Mark Reynolds being whisked away, I felt selfishly comforted. The boundaries of a moral universe were being brutally traced, and I belonged firmly within them.

*

Home finances forced me to go from part-time to full-time at the university, which in turn meant that we placed Jemima into daycare two days a week. This freed up Brad to chase more work in between his freelance gigs. My parents minded her on Tuesdays, and we employed my sweet-tempered cousins to nanny her for a day also. I worked from home a day a week and convinced myself I could complete tasks while Jemima played with her blocks, or if she napped, but in reality those hours were sucked up with small-person demands, and I wound up compressing a full-time workload into four long days plus snatches of time on weekends. Like many mothers, I was at my desk at 4 am each day to squeeze in a couple of hours before Jemima awoke.

Jemima's daycare was at a cottage on campus near my office. It had five rooms, one for each of the age groups – possums, cockatoos, wombats, echidnas, koalas – and a colourful outside area with climbing equipment and spots to dig dirt and plant carrots. Jemima was two years old and hungry for playmates, so mostly the drop-offs in the mornings weren't traumatic, although herding her out the door of our apartment required heroic patience: she wants to wear the pink dress with the hearts but it's grubby, and threatens to tantrum until I wriggle it onto her; she must brush her teeth but she is a cheetah that creeps on four legs, so I lie almost prostrate straining to reach a mini toothbrush into her rosebud mouth; she has lost her blue shoe and we hunt and hunt until it's found jammed down the side of the sofa; she sees an orange flower in the garden that wasn't there yesterday and skips across to study it. As I hurried her along, I imagined a seraphic nurturer and saw how horribly I was falling short. The pressures of my job and of mothering combined to form an anvil-like weight on my chest.

The daycare hosted children of academics: geographers, historians, marine biologists, engineers. Colleagues and I arrived to collect our kids, exchanging weary glances, appreciating what the day had contained: meetings about redesigning the teaching curriculum; meetings outlining the number of books and research papers we must be publishing; meetings with co-researchers as we wrote grant applications; sessions with our diligent PhD students and their thorny thesis chapters; the assessment of detailed ethics applications; teaching back-to-back tutorials while placating undergraduates about their final essays. We would arrive home with our children, execute the bath, dinner, bedtime routine, and then flip open our laptops to continue working.

There were days when it went wrong. It was Space Day, and I had assembled a dress-up outfit for Jemima: she was the sun, with yellow clothing and crepe-paper rays. When I dropped her off, steering her towards her favourite carer, she pushed her face into my thigh, refusing to emerge. I had to deliver a 9 am lecture.

'You'll have fun making the planets,' I told her, but she gripped my leg.

As I tried unknotting myself, her nails caught my black stockings and I felt the tickle of the ladder run.

'I have to go. I love you. You'll be okay. I'll see you this afternoon,' and I ran down the hall.

'Mummeee! Mummee!' she sobbed in fury and despair.

Outside I numbed myself, examining the long, jagged rip, like a cartoon lightning strike, revealing my unshaven leg. In high heels, I half-jogged to Woolworths for a pair of tights, and twenty minutes later I strode into the lecture theatre, breathless and sweaty, where 200 students were filing in.

That afternoon Jemima showed me the papier-mâché Saturn the class had made with its tutu-skirt for rings. But then she struck a warrior pose: legs bent and separated, one arm outstretched aimed at me, the other squeezed to her chest.

'Pahw! I kill you!' she said.

A gun. She must have seen the other kids, the ones with older siblings, shooting one another. I pointed to her extended arm and asked what it was. She paused. She had no word for it.

'It's a pipe,' she said finally. 'When I press a button, fire shoots out the end of it and you die.'

'Oh,' I said. 'What a shame.'

There were additional challenges. Jemima brought home an array of colds and stomach bugs, and the three of us were ill for seventeen weeks straight. A friend reassured me that within two years our family would become bionic. In the meantime, while our thriving daughter conquered everything in forty-eight hours, Brad and I staggered from week to week, dragged down by viruses and resentment.

We quarrelled more than usual, fights sparked by disagreements over the division of household labour, which quickly blazed with thoughtless words and hurt. On Mother's Day we had a row over the deployment of a simile. I'd been reading a memoir that had compared the job of a working mother to that of an air traffic controller. When I told Brad, he replied: 'Yeah, but an air traffic controller is responsible for thousands of lives.' I archly pointed out that the writer's use of language was not homologous but analogous, that metaphors and similes deliberately yank together *different* things in order to make descriptions of experience more vivid. Now we were both pissed off. Jemima watched us, wide-eyed, absorbing the catastrophe. In an attempt to provide a salve, I turned to her and supplied a running commentary: 'Mummy and Daddy are so angry with one another and we are having an argument. People argue sometimes. Don't worry, we'll make up soon. We're just so furious and we're finding it hard to stop. Gosh it's hard though when we're so mad, isn't it. Look! See! Now Daddy and I are giving one another a big hug and saying sorry.'

That night, we lay in bed and sourly, silently replayed the fight.

*

On a Friday at four o'clock my mobile phone rang.

'Is that Dr Rossmanith?' an elderly man's voice asked.

I instantly recognised it. It belonged to the judge who had sentenced that woman. He apologised for the delay in contacting me, explaining that he was retiring from the bench and that today was his last day of work, but that if I could be in his chambers in thirty minutes he would be happy to chat with me.

As it so happened, I was in a café on Phillip Street directly opposite his building. I scribbled down questions, cursing myself for my unpreparedness and for my knock-about outfit: a swingy, black-and-white stretch-cotton dress that now appeared worn and shapeless.

At the Law Courts building, a hideous chimney-looking structure, I took the lift up and was shown into His Honour's chambers.

Without his judicial robes and wig, without the ritual trappings, the judge looked smaller and sprightlier than he'd been in court. He was comfortably seated in his office that had been stripped of books and everything else, the walls of empty wooden shelves exposed. He apologised that he could not offer me coffee 'because everything is packed away'. But not everything was packed. Sitting on the large table where we sat either side facing one another was the solid tome of the *Sentencing Act*. It looked lonely with the weight of authority.

I asked him about the woman he had sentenced, and how he could tell if someone feels remorse.

'It was obvious in her case,' he began, 'because the moment she got out of the car she attempted to lift the front of the car off the person underneath, as did the poor victim's brother. She was in a *terrible* state up on the road when a nurse came along. She was pulling her hair out and she was in a *highly distressed* condition. When she gave an interview with the police she was in an extremely distressed state. She told lies. Now, very often if you tell lies, it's inconsistent with remorse, but in her case I think that she just didn't want to accept what she had done. It is not unusual for people, particularly if they have done something instantaneous and terrible, to refuse to accept responsibility for it. The young man's family always saw that as a lack of remorse. And I can understand that. But there was also clear evidence from the jail authorities of her constant anguish about what she'd done: medical reports of clinical nurses and clinical psychologists who were treating her bipolar disorder. But part of it too was that she was a mother, she had a son who she loved and who she wanted to have back with her, and yet she'd killed somebody else's son. I have no doubt in her case that there was real remorse.'

A lawyerly response. He had even built in, and rejected, a counter-argument ('She told lies').

I raised the fact of the woman's demeanour in court. She looked disturbed. Did that mean anything?

'Yes, but who can tell?' he snapped back. 'Some people can be very good actors. The distress could be about what's going to happen to *her*, and not remorse. The distress and pain can be about the fact that she knows she's going to get a very significant sentence because she was convicted of murder. Very often it's hard to tell whether it's remorse for committing the crime, remorse as to the effect of the crime upon the offender's family or remorse for their own situation. I determine whether or not the remorse is genuine by considering what people *do* after the offence rather than what they say about it.'

The psychological reports. 'A psychiatrist told me that remorse is untestable,' I said.

In this case, the reports submitted to the court were from clinical psychologists responsible for the woman's ongoing treatment, explained the judge. They attested to her constant anguish. Such reports 'were not based on a one-off encounter with a psychiatrist or a psychologist who was being paid to write a report'. And they did not constitute the only evidence. This, he felt, was critical.

On cue he opened the *Sentencing Act* and read out a list: 'Section 3A says the purposes for which a court may impose a sentence are "To ensure that the accused is adequately punished. To prevent crime by deterring the offender and others. To protect the community. To promote rehabilitation. To make the offender accountable for his actions. To denounce the conduct of the offender. To recognise the harm done to the victim." That's common law. The common law sees those things as the purpose of punishment. Remorse is a significant factor in determining how much punishment should be aimed at "denouncing" or "retribution", and how much should be aimed at "rehabilitation".'

It was a fusion of the Old Testament with the modern dream of self-transformation.

With that he was done. He showed me to the foyer and we said goodbye.

So, I thought to myself as I stepped out onto Phillip Street and walked to the bus stop, *that woman's twisted body I was so fixated on, the way she wept and tugged at her suit jacket, counted for little when it came to the judge's assessment.*

A couple of days later, I had lunch with my friend Ruth, a former criminal defence lawyer who knew quite a bit about that murder case, and who listened, eyebrows raised, as I described the woman's desperate figure in court.

Ruth shook her head. She reached across and took my hand.

'Kate, when that woman was on remand in jail awaiting the trial, she had come off drugs and had gained ten kilos. That suit you say she was wearing? She was pulling at it because it didn't bloody *fit* her.'

II

JUDGMENT

8

We moved from the apartment at the beach to a house in Sydney's north. Jemima watched her world coming apart – we dismantled the beds and packed her toys in boxes. When two big sweaty men trudged in, took our things, and carried them downstairs to their big white truck, she howled. Brad and I soothed her with promises of a garden and a cubby, but 'home' is not an abstract thing, certainly not for a three-year-old. Take away the red sofa that's good for bouncing, and the short wooden table where you spill milk and no one gets cross; take away the sensation of your little legs bounding up the narrow hallway, the smell of the hessian floor mats and the sea. What is left?

The new place was very quiet. It felt far away, which it was, according to Brad who missed the surf and the cosmopolitanism of our coastal life. In the week we arrived, he made three trips to our old suburb for no other reason than to remind himself it was still there. The novelist William Gibson wrote about how air travel can cause a kind of soul delay: how, when we are on a plane, our souls can't move as quickly and so remain leagues behind us, 'being reeled in on some ghostly umbilical down the vanished wake of the plane', and how we must wait for them to catch up. The same might be said of moving house, even if it's only a 45-minute drive.

We had moved to be closer to my university, to Jemima's daycare, and to cheaper rent. You could lease a house with a yard here for two-thirds of the price in the east or inner west. We put on Beatles songs and the three of us danced around like loons in the airy bedrooms, into the 1950s bathroom with its dusky-pink bath, and through to the living rooms with views of the bush.

Our neighbours were ninety and seventy years old and lived in weatherboard cottages they'd built half a century ago. They smiled at Jemima who searched for fairies among the gardenias and native violets.

The area is one of the wettest in Sydney, receiving more rain than most, which has been explained by its particular weather feature: the 'orographic uplift'; it's just close enough to the coast to get the ocean air and just high enough to convert clouds into precipitation. The suburb is a thousand greens. Olive, jade, pistachio, emerald, lime, chartreuse. Frog-green lawns with rose beds. Native bush gardens in military tones.

Our house was in a valley. Gum trees and pines – 50, 60 metres tall – surrounded us like ancient, benevolent megaflora, and, everywhere, birds: sulphur-crested cockatoos, crimson rosellas, kookaburras, brush turkeys, eastern whipbirds, pied currawongs and powerful owls. We also happened to be next to the Hills District, Australia's 'bible belt'. We drove past churches with signs out the front: 'God is building a home' and 'He who is faithful and just will forgive us our sins and cleanse us from all unrighteousness'.

There was another reason we had moved: I still wasn't sleeping properly. I'd have the odd restful night but mostly I carried in me a fathomless unease. Perhaps the eucalypts would help to quiet the soul. At night in the new house, during the cold hours when hollow thoughts presented themselves, I prayed for serenity. I yearned for an encounter with the divine, wanting to believe in a monotheistic god, and in angels, but never in God's divine will.

A year earlier, we had had Jemima baptised. Brad had taken some convincing, he couldn't see the point, and I'd endeavoured to articulate why I felt so strongly about it. It had seemed important to bring together our family and to welcome our toddler into God's arms. She was baptised in the Uniting Church by a minister who was a close friend of my parents. He was committed to social justice, including Indigenous land rights, and his approach to Christianity combined ancient history, psychology and eastern philosophy. His theological orientation was what had drawn my mother and father to the Uniting Church two decades ago when they were in their late forties and searching for a spiritual community. On the day of the baptism we dressed Jemima in a cream-coloured slip that my great-grandmother had made my grandmother in the 1930s. During the service we placed her tiny feet in a tray of soil. It was a mixture of special soil we had gathered: soil from the garden of the house in which I grew up, soil from Brad's childhood home, soil from outside the hospital where she was born, and soil from our own garden. We wished for our child a meaningful connection to history, land and place.

The Christian philosopher and theologian Paul Tillich wrote that it takes existential courage to face the three-fold anxiety of human existence: fate and death, emptiness and meaninglessness, guilt and condemnation. Acquiring such courage, I felt, necessitated teasing apart, examining and suturing together my own extreme and anodyne experiences, and those of my family, to make sense of a life.

Despite being christened Catholic, I was raised with no particular religion. Matters of theology hummed alongside me rather than within me – they were questions to ponder rather than rites to enact – and it is perhaps why I have never grasped the mechanics of almighty absolution. My mother's mother was a little girl when, in 1929, she and her family migrated to Sydney from Calabria, Italy; my grandfather was in his late teens when he migrated in 1938 from Catania, Sicily. Mum's parents met indirectly by way of the Australian internment camps during the war: 'suspect' males – in this case, Italian – were arrested and transported to compounds in towns such as Hay and Orange in inland New South Wales, or were sent to the Northern Territory to work on the roads, or to Tasmania to help build the Butlers Gorge Power Station. Mum's grandfather was among those men interned. While in the camps, he played chess with a fellow internee – a tender-hearted man much younger than himself, with Clark Gable's looks and charm, who would eventually become his son-in-law.

Mum's parents bought and ran a delicatessen in Panania, a working-class suburb in south-west Sydney, and they lived behind the shop with their rapidly expanding family. The arrival home meant walking into the deli, past the cool room with its cold meats and blocky cheeses, and through to the basic living quarters. The place had a sliver of soil out the back in which Mum's father grew sweet peas.

Mum went to a Catholic school (where the wearing of ponytails was banned because the hairdo looked provocative), and attended a small suburban church nearby. Dressed in her frothy white frock for her First Holy Communion in 1956, she knelt before the priest, opened her mouth and received Christ. A nun told her that if she felt like throwing up, she must vomit in a spot where no one would tread because, remember, it is Jesus's body. Mum, seven years old, organised it in her mind: were she ever to fall ill after eating the wafer, she would crawl under the school building to virgin soil.

Her first communion meant her first confession. She had rehearsed the lines, but when she entered the chamber she felt frightened by the dark and the priest. She invented sins, and she continued to do this at every confession for the next ten years because, according to her, she was a good girl. She told priest after priest that she was disobedient, which she figured was the sort of sin children committed. (One of Mum's younger brothers was more creative: when he was seven, he confessed to committing adultery. 'With whom?' asked the priest, to which the boy replied after a confused pause: 'With my brother.') Mum approached confession the way she approached teeth-brushing, which is to say, by rote. The one tantalising element was predicting what penance she would receive. This all depended on which priest she happened to get, and what mood he was in. She usually received three Hail Marys. Once, she received a whole rosary. As she sat on the pew counting the beads, she wondered if she lacked the insight to recognise her own evil.

As a young teenager, Mum attended Mass in the school hall and went on school retreats where the girls chanted supplications to the saints. She experienced her spirit lifting, and wondered whether this was a calling to become a nun. When she alluded to the possibility, her father told her not to think about it. To him, a nun's life was one of deprivation and sacrifice, and he wanted his only daughter to study, and to have a good life, which included marrying and having babies. He needn't have worried about her earlier fervent devotion. By the time Mum was seventeen, she was questioning what she saw as the elements of Catholic faith: the male authority, the emphasis on reward after death, the judgment and condemnation from the pulpit. Most difficult for her was the exclusivity that did not allow those of other faiths to partake of communion, a practice that was at total odds with what went on in her family home, where everyone was welcome at the table.

When Mum was in her late teens, her family left the back of the shop and moved into the two-storey house they'd built on land in Carlingford, an up-and-coming area in western Sydney. They had a front garden and a back garden and a solid front door with a brass knocker, behind which they could play Beethoven at top volume.

When she attended Mass, she watched herself and the congregation as if for the first time – the standing, the kneeling, the hands crossed on chest, the prayers, the candles, the incense, the cramped confessional chamber – and she reviewed her lifetime of devotion with astonishment. And, anyway, by then she had started university, had begun dating classmates, and had met my father.

Dad was her second-year university maths tutor. He taught her computing and calculus. When they first set eyes on one another, each had the overwhelming sense: *I know him*; *I know her*. My father's strong sense of propriety meant that it was only an entire year later, when he knew she would never again be in his class, that he asked her out. She was walking across campus to the library when she bumped into him. When she told him she was on her way to borrow books for her younger brother who was doing a school assignment about Aboriginal Australians, he said that, if she was interested, he could take her to West Head to see the Aboriginal rock art and engravings there. That Saturday he arrived at her parents' house at two o'clock, where my mother was inside scrambling to finish sewing a green blouse she'd made for the outing. My grandmother greeted Dad at the door. Mum attached the final button. Then the two of them drove off in his Volkswagen Beetle, they toured the carvings, and on the way back, Dad stopped at a flower stall and bought her some carnations. To this day my father says that, when he first entered my grandparents' house, when he smelt smells of European cooking, and when he encountered Mum's loud, loving family, he felt he'd come home.

At night I lay awake in our new place, with its new smells and new contours, and considered how the architecture of my family was lopsided. On my mother's side, dozens of uncles, aunts, cousins and grandparents – and the narratives they tell and have told – formed muscular structures of genealogy. But Dad would not discuss with us his family of origin. My father's side was almost shapeless.

From conversations with Mum, I had the impression that Dad's religious faith was not a result of his family upbringing but of song.

When my father was little and still in Vienna, his father disappeared and he never saw him again. In 1953, by the time Dad was ten, his mother could not see a future for her family in Europe. People worried about the territorial ambition of the Soviet Union; the Iron Curtain was advancing westward. My grandmother abandoned her home and everything that made her who she was, and brought her two children to Australia. In Sydney, dismembered by a new language and a new land, she was at a loss for how to reconfigure herself. She worked long hours, and therefore sent her girl and boy away to live in hostels.

For two years, Dad lived in a hostel run by a Methodist minister and his wife in Pendle Hill, an area near Parramatta known for its cotton-spinning mill. The place was one of fifty or so institutions nationally that took in children as part of child migration schemes. The twenty-three British boys alongside whom my father boarded were among thousands of poor or orphaned children sent from the UK to Australia to populate the country with 'good, white stock'; many of those children would, decades later, as part of a parliamentary inquiry, speak of the physical, sexual and psychological abuse and neglect they were subjected to in those homes, and how, when they eventually grew up and had their own children, they were filled with anger and despair because it was beyond their capabilities to cope with a family.

Not all children suffered cruelty. Some were treated well, and my father says that he was one of the fortunate ones, although I am unsure whether to believe him. In Vienna he'd been a wild child, always in strife, and he maintains that, had he not come to Australia and been forced to find a way to survive, his fate would have likely been that of so many other fatherless boys: prison. A photo in the National Archives shows sixteen boys, two men and a woman, standing together on the flat, baked land of the Pendle Hill property, the hostel-house a monolith in the background. It was taken in 1953, the year my father was sent there. He isn't in the photo, although it's hard to tell. The image is indistinct. The boys just all look like little boys, in their pale shirts and shorts. To use the possessive pronoun, however, is misleading: there was no 'their'. The children didn't own anything. Everything belonged to the house. After each laundry wash they would grab whatever was in reach, jostling for clothes that fit.

Dad had arrived at the hostel speaking only German, the language of the enemy, but immediately began to learn English and was celebrated for his quick acquisition of it. He attended two church services every Sunday, scripture stories weaving themselves around him to form a sort of invisible shelter. But it was the singing that brought him closest to God. On Friday nights, the group sang Presbyterian and Methodist choruses, and, as he sang those sustained notes and perfect fourths, he felt his spirit soar.

The hostel boys performed at Sydney Town Hall at a fundraising event for a Protestant organisation. My father sang a solo. He must have sounded angelic, because a man in the audience was struck by his voice, and arranged for Dad to audition as a chorister and student for St Andrew's Cathedral School. Dad knew of the St Andrew's choir. He'd heard it once when it toured the state, and the force of the music had stayed with him. At his audition, he stood in front of the choirmaster and began to sing songs of the choir. He hadn't the words, but, on listening to those St Andrew's singers all those months ago, the melodies had embedded themselves in him and he offered the vocals back to his assessor like a heavenly call-and-response. He was awarded a choir school scholarship that paid his tuition fees.

The directness of Anglicanism appealed to Dad, whose life circumstances fostered in him a headstrong independence coupled with a furious privacy. He was familiar with the famous passage in Luke: how Jesus was teaching when some men approached carrying a paralysed man but couldn't fit in the door through the crowd, so they lowered the man from the roof and set him before Jesus; how, when Jesus saw their faith, he said: 'Your sins are forgiven'; how the scribes and Pharisees considered this blasphemous, for Judaism acclaimed God as the source of health and illness. Sickness was a divine-mandated punishment for individual and communal sins, those you had committed and those your parents and their parents had committed too. Jesus responded: 'Which is easier? To say, "Your sins are forgiven", or to say, "Get up and walk"? The Son of Man has authority on the earth to forgive sins.' To the paralytic, Jesus said: 'I tell you, get up, pick up your mat, and go home'; immediately the man rose up and walked.

My father didn't take these stories at face value, but as necessarily existing within vast, contextual flows, and he was always reading ancient history, fascinated by the cultural and cosmological understandings of the time. I would watch him as he studied the scriptures, his finger tracing the tiny print as he made meaning of old words. He tracked down the Greek word for 'sin' (*hamartia*, 'missing the mark', as in a badly aimed spear throw) and the word for 'forgive' (*aphie'mi*, 'send away', 'dispatch', or 'set free'). I liked the thought that we could be set free from our sickness, set free from failure.

When my sister and I were born, Mum still felt the pull to Catholicism, so we were christened by the priest who had married my parents, a gentle man who was broad in understanding and belief. When my brother arrived, my parents turned elsewhere, and the baby was welcomed into the Kingdom of God via a Protestant church near our house. Dad took my sister and me to that church when we were small. The walk there was short: ten minutes if you had grown-man legs, twice that if you had little-girl ones. As we held hands and skipped across the highway, under the railway bridge and up the steep stone steps of Hill Street, Dad, who had an infatuation with parables, told us a story he'd invented called Butty Button.

Butty and the other buttons lived on Jacket. One day Jacket left home for an outing.

'Jump into your button holes,' Jacket told the buttons.

The buttons climbed into their holes, all except for Butty. As Jacket walked out the door and down the road, Butty flipped and flapped. Jacket walked past a bush. *Snap!* Butty was ripped from Jacket. Torn right off!

'Help!' cried Butty, who was caught between two thin branches. 'Jacket! Come back!'

Maybe Jacket will forget about me, Butty thought, and began to cry. Jacket looked down and saw that Butty was missing. He rushed back, retracing his steps, searching high in the branches, and on the ground.

'Butty! Where *are* you?' yelled Jacket.

When he finally found the little button, he hugged him to his chest. At home, Butty was stitched back onto Jacket. From then on, whenever Butty heard Jacket say, 'Jump into your button holes', he was the first to climb in.

As I grew older, I became incensed by the story's conformist moral. I now realise that it wasn't about obedience so much as dread: Dad was Jacket and we were the buttons he was terrified of losing.

When I was twelve, he stopped taking us to church and we stopped going. Theology and spirituality were around us at home, and these things I remember more vividly than Sunday School tales of donkeys, lambs and lepers: books by Marcus Borg, and by Teilhard de Chardin on my parents' bookshelf; a print of Rembrandt's *The Return of the Prodigal Son*, on the sideboard in the lounge room; Dad's humming of hymns and German Christmas carols; the veil my mother wore at her First Holy Communion hanging from the bedroom mantelpiece, alongside her mother's rosary beads, a reminder of early innocence and devotion; and, above Mum's desk, poems by Rabindranath Tagore, Constantine Cavafy, Julian of

Norwich, Gerard Manley Hopkins ('The world is charged with the grandeur of God'), among others, including this one by the Persian mystical poet Rumi:

> Come, come whoever you are,
> Wanderer, worshipper, lover of leaving
> It doesn't matter. Ours is not a caravan of despair.
> Come, even if you have broken your vows a thousand times.
> Come, come, yet again, come.

My parents believe in a relationship with God; that, by turning to God, we are restored and made whole. But what they call 'God' they might also refer to as the Divine, the Great Mystery, the Breath of Life: there is an 'as-if' quality, a recognition that they are searching for something beyond themselves. I wanted to feel as they did: held by this larger thing. I wanted to find a language for it, to fold myself into it. But my mother says: 'words are pale and inconsequential against the great reach'.

9

In the new house, I would find Brad leaning against a window frame in the lounge room, his back to me. He would be looking up at a tree or at the sky. He wasn't taking in the outside world, the way one might take in a painting. His restless looking-out was an itching to escape – at least this was what I deduced.

He and I had grown expert at not having the conversation that had to be had, the one where we talked about loss, and longing.

In the early years of our relationship, before we got married, before Jemima, the question of a baby had hung over us. I was approaching thirty, next thing you know I'd rounded the bend, and I pressed him again and again: when would we begin trying? He ducked and dodged until one day I told him that I loved him but that love wasn't enough, and that he needed to make a decision: if he wasn't ready to have a child in the next couple of years, I was not the partner for him. I kissed him, packed a bag and left our apartment to stay at a girlfriend's place where I set about swaddling my heart. A week later Brad came to me and said that he couldn't imagine living his life without me, that I was his home, and that, whenever I was ready to take the leap to have a baby, he'd leap with me.

Now, instead of us communicating as we used to, I silently created a mural of backstory for him that might explain his behaviour: the passing of youth, dreams shut away in a drawer. Sometimes, I'd cautiously approach him to touch his arm or give him a hug, thinking perhaps the physical contact would draw him out, but he called these advances of mine 'hovering' and they annoyed him. When he said it – 'You're hovering' – the hurt zapped through me. Before I could question him about what he was doing and why, he would grab his keys and announce he was 'going for a drive'. He'd climb into his most cherished possession, a shiny black Volkswagen, and zoom off, probably to a beach somewhere to watch the ocean and imagine himself swimming towards infinity.

It was what I had always known him as: a swimmer. We'd grown up in the same neighbourhood and had gone to primary school together, Brad being two years ahead of me. Both he and his younger sisters were champion swimmers, flying up and down the pool at carnivals, representing the school at district and state competitions. That all three siblings were also tall and striking looking had the rest of us regarding them as water gods.

He and I had got together in our late twenties after running into one another at Bondi Beach markets. He'd done a bachelor's degree in music and had worked as a jazz saxophonist before re-enrolling to study science. He'd just returned from living in London for four years. Now he was working in film. I told him about my own travels and the PhD I was writing, and he suggested we meet for a coffee. The following week at a café we talked for hours, talk that felt deep and wild and beautiful.

What struck me that day, and in the years afterwards, were his intelligence, his humour, his work ethic and his honesty. He spoke plainly about his life, which freed me to speak plainly about mine. No posturing, no hiding. It was important to him, as it was to me, to cut straight to the heart of things, whether we were discussing creativity and design, politics, philosophy, science; our respective disappointments and struggles professionally and personally; or our families of origin, with whom we were close. When we were together, our questions and formulations about the world and one another seemed to pierce life's nuclei, which in turn energised the air around us.

When you meet someone who stimulates you so completely, you feel two things that can't possibly exist concomitantly but somehow do: one, exhilaration that intensifies the colours and contours of existence; the other, a far-reaching peace, a sublime calm that comes with truly seeing a person, and with being seen.

Brad needed those drives alone, but they also fortified the space between us. While I knew that our marital situation was common to the point of cliché – one partner retreating, the other seeking out connection – this knowledge did little to allay my dolour. 'Kate is compelling. She's *so compelling*,' Brad had announced during his speech at our wedding. And yet now I'd disappeared, all but vanished from his view. Neither he nor I was deliberately hiding from one another; it's that we were each snared in our own tangle of feeling. I wanted so much for him to walk back through the door and for those skeins that shrouded us to tumble to the floor.

*

When I asked them about people's remorse, the judges I was interviewing talked of 'spontaneous displays of emotion'. There was 'genuine remorse', they told me, and then there was superficial, cynical, qualified, manufactured, confined, feigned, perfunctory remorse. When an offender's remorse was profound, a judge could feel it from across the courtroom.

Their descriptions sounded metaphysical. The etymology of remorse (*re-mordere*) means 'to bite again', referring to the bite it holds on the conscience and on the spirit. I knew that judges weren't Jesus, their job was to dispense justice, but I couldn't decouple Christian theology from the courts. For centuries, remorse in the courts was about the afterlife of the spirit; convicted criminals were expected to express remorse because it secured their spiritual wellbeing: when people were sentenced to death, repentance saved their souls.

No one ever said it, but soul-saving continued to preoccupy the common law. Three elderly judges I spoke with wept when they recounted to me displays of people's remorse. One referred to it as a 'Road to Damascus' experience. I imagined a person's inner essence flooding the courtroom. Souls bursting through skin. A prosecutor told me that the courts were in the business of knowing people, and that judges and juries needed to 'connect with offenders on an ethereal level'. He believed that cross-examination was the mechanism for eliciting truthfulness. Whenever he cross-examined the accused person in the witness box, he was being a 'sounding board', the way that a backboard of a piano or violin reflects the sound. The accused provided the answers, but he, the prosecutor, was amplifying the sound so that the jury and judge could make an assessment. The prosecutor was magnifying and communicating the muted truth, amplifying a person's true self.

One night I switched on the heater in the study and sifted through photocopies of nineteenth-century newspaper articles, among which were details of a famous 1827 case in New South Wales. An Aboriginal man, 'Tommy', had been convicted by the Supreme Court of murdering a white stockman near Georges Plains, and had been executed. The case is well known because it was the first test of *terra nullius* in Australia: the decision indicated that Aboriginal people were subject to English law only where the incident concerned both natives and settlers, the rationale being that Aboriginal tribal groups already operated under their own legal systems. I was interested in the case because of the strange way in which the colonists imposed on Tommy what a conscience was.

According to the reports, Tommy came upon two stockmen on a property in Bathurst, with whom he ate a meal before spending the night with his own family 200 yards from the white men's hut. In the morning Tommy returned and murdered one of the men. The other fellow found the victim lying in a small fire, his head broken and burnt, his right arm placed across his heart, and the fellow and his team tracked 'the blacks' until they located Tommy, who was with two women – one heavily pregnant – as well as with a little boy and a baby. Upon seeing his pursuers, Tommy let out a 'loud shriek'.

Tommy was caught and put on trial. Through an interpreter, he pleaded his innocence, maintaining that it was another man who had killed the stockman. The jury retired for five minutes and returned a verdict of guilty. The judge sentenced him to death.

One newspaper cited the work of a doctor who argued that inflicting bodily or mental injury on a guilty person 'would teach him to be aware how he inflicted the like injury on his neighbour', and that the savage would feel guilt, and would become a proper subject of punitive justice. The Chief Justice proclaimed that Tommy 'was very conscious of having violated a law in slaying a fellow creature, or why scream out and fly at the approach of a pursuer?' The article concluded that Tommy's shriek 'proved the existence of *remorse*', and that therefore Tommy deserved to be 'brought to condign punishment'.

Tommy's shriek had undone him. The article was saying that his conscience, through the scream (if indeed that's *why* he screamed), bore witness to his sin. It was a manifestation of his *soul*.

When clergymen visited him in his cell, Tommy persistently denied guilt. On the final day of December 1827, he was one of five men due to be hanged in Bathurst. The other four, all white, had been convicted of robbery.

> [T]hey mounted, one after another, the scaffold-board, and were mustered and ranged by the hangman, who fitted the halters speedily [. . .]; it was an awful site [sic]. There were five human beings standing on the brink of, and ready to be hurled into eternity, without a hope [. . .] of reprieve.

Just before the executioner was about to do his duty, an argument flared between a Protestant minister and a Catholic chaplain about Tommy's spirit. The chaplain asked Tommy if he wished to be saved. Tommy made no reply, but the minister who was nearby reprimanded the chaplain for the gross impropriety of administering the ordinance of baptism, as the condemned was a heathen, destitute of all knowledge of Christianity, the minister repeating: 'He that *believeth* and is baptised shall *be saved*.' The chaplain replied, 'We baptise infants who do not understand the nature of baptism; he is in the same state,' and immediately made the sign of the cross on Tommy's forehead with the consecrated water. Then each of the five men was hanged.

I returned the articles to the stack of papers on my desk and slipped back into bed. There was a sliver of light from the streetlamp squinting through the wooden blinds, and the dark shape of the ceiling fan hung above me like a suspended 'x' for 'error'.

The criminal courts figured themselves as soul-savers and truth-seekers, but sometimes they were simply impressing on another person what a human being is, and should be. Humans and their souls were different things to different people, I thought to myself. The heat from Brad, sleeping, moved lightly across my skin.

10

Magistrates sit at benches in stuffy courtrooms in Waverley, the CBD, North Sydney; in Bankstown, Ryde, Gosford. Some wear quick ponytails, rogue wisps tucked behind their ears; others have furrowed foreheads and greying countenances.

Law-breakers have been summonsed. They huddle together in the public seating. Pretty police officers with bobby-pin patterns in their hair stand at the back, while lawyers in royal purple ties mumble to their clients. Plastic clocks, old and yellowing, hang like afterthoughts from grubby noticeboards. Minutes crawl by.

The magistrates announce people's names ('Matter of Trevor Williams', 'Matter of Rebecca North', 'Matter of George Lord'), directing them to various courtrooms in the various buildings. Everyone holds bits of paper; some carry thick wads of the stuff, using their fingers as bookmarks to separate the bundles. Court lists are drawn up. Agitated people file in and out and find their correct places. The stage management is complicated for one magistrate whose swivel chair requires mending: each time she hoists it up it sinks back down below the bench until all spectators can see is a neck-less head talking to them, like Winnie in Beckett's *Happy Days*.

A groomed woman from the North Shore stands, chin thrust out. Charged with mid-range PCA, Prescribed Concentration of Alcohol, she implores the magistrate not to revoke her driver's licence.

'Everyone here at court today for drink driving offences has tales to tell,' explains the magistrate. 'Many people are of good character, but this does not detract from the serious nature of the offence.'

The woman is fined several hundred dollars and she is disqualified from holding a licence for six months.

A bulky bloke from the Australian Defence Force drove drunk and injured two of his passengers.

'He feels terrible about what happened,' booms the man's counsel in a Shakespearian voice. 'He is distressed about the injury to his friends, and about his lapse in judgment. He has completed the Traffic Offenders Program, and has got insight into the offence. It will *not* occur again!'

'I should consider sending you to jail for twelve months and fining you three thousand dollars,' a magistrate tells the offender. 'This is what the community expects.' But because of the man's participation in the traffic program, he is only fined $1000 and disqualified from driving for eighteen months.

A young man rode his motorbike down the wrong side of a main road. He ignored the police who pursued him and sped away.

'My client didn't realise that there was a police pursuit,' says the lawyer.

The magistrate won't have a bar of it, and denounces his 'outrageous behaviour'. The young man's licence was not confiscated at the time of the incident; with theatrical flourish it is confiscated now. The offender produces it from his wallet. The court officer pounds over and seizes it from him.

A grandmotherly woman has been charged with mid-range drink-driving. Her counsel appeals to the court: his client needs her licence to help her pregnant daughter and to visit her infirm mother;

she has completed a recovery program for addictive behaviour; she volunteers for community service; and she suffers from depression.

'Most people in the room today are of exemplary character,' says the magistrate. 'For many, it's their first offence. But the offence is serious.'

The woman is fined $600 and she is disqualified from driving for six months.

Five hours pass. Each magistrate will process scores of matters.

Sitting watching it all, I wonder about the shattering boredom of dealing with the same types of offences day in, day out. The responsibility of having to treat each matter one at a time.

Later I ask magistrates about this. They joke: *if only we could implement a bulk-sentencing practice for drink-driving offences, dividing people into low-range, mid-range, high-range, P-plater, second-time offender.*

But no, every person is an individual.

Magistrates tell you that they handle the onerous workload by recycling different speeches. They have got their speech for the old guy; their speech for the young guy; their *It's not rocket science* speech; their *You can't count your drinks* speech; their *You might not think you are lucky, but you are* speech; their *You could have killed someone* speech. They've got them all.

*

We had been in the house for six months when the rain arrived and stayed for ten days. We listened to the rattle of steamy summer showers, grateful we'd left behind our cramped apartment and that Jemima had space indoors to run and dance.

During breaks in the weather, we crept outside to explore the garden. The wet brought spiders, hundreds of them. Brad found a community of red-backs in the garage. Among the branches along the path we caught sight of abdomens, each with eight delicate spikes, hanging there on fine webs, patiently hunting. Near the front gate I watched a brown, leggy thing zip across its lacy trap and wrap a blowfly victim until the parcel was mummified, heavy and ripe.

The rain brought other insects too. Jemima studied swirling ant patterns. When the black texta marks marched up the wall near her cubbyhouse, she squealed, 'How do they *do* that?' and she discovered mozzies, moths and ladybugs executing the same fantastical feat. As the brickwork around us bristled with creatures, Brad and I told her that if we were tiny, we would walk up walls too.

It should have been scientifically delightful to contemplate the relation between an object's size and the fundamental interactions of the universe – how, for example, gravitational force is negligible for very small animals – but thinking about weightlessness made me shudder. Teensy things, the way they are dominated by surface force and attraction – the way they can *stick* – were dangerous.

For two years I had been circling the courts. I'd watched and listened, again and again, to accounts of crime, judgment and regret. Sometimes I found myself referring to these various things as 'stories'. But really they weren't. They didn't yet possess the necessary mass to be classed as such. I thought they were properly, densely formed in my mind, but they weren't.

Early one Friday afternoon I caused a car accident. I had just left a court session during which a genial offender was being sentenced for drug supply. He'd sat in the dock that was encased by a perspex partition, like a little plastic cell. His wife in the public seating pined for her husband, and during a break in proceedings, she approached him but was told by guards to stand one metre from the enclosure.

As I was driving Brad's car in bumper-to-bumper traffic, having swapped cars with him for the day, I mulled over the prescriptive positioning of bodies in the courts. I must have glanced away. I rear-ended the car in front. The soft, easy feeling of Brad's bonnet merging with the stranger's white Holden Commodore was discordant with the hard, loud sound of crushing metal.

Brad's car stopped dead and so did I, hands over my face. A witness slotted the front number plate through my driver window. When I could finally make my body make the car move, I joined the Commodore down a side street. Brad's vehicle had a creased nose. The other car had taken the brunt. Its owner, a rangy young man – Rob was his name – climbed out and stood next to it. I approached him – 'I'm *so* sorry' – and we inspected the damage. The back of his car was okay, but the front was busted. The collision had pushed it into the spare wheel of the four-wheel drive in front of him (that car was un-scraped and had driven off), and now his ruined radiator leaked puddles on the bitumen.

Rob's Commodore required towing, which meant we had to report the accident. I told the police officer on the phone that I'd caused a minor car accident. Indifferent, he said he would send around 'the first available car'.

I phoned Brad. He asked calm, pointed questions about the state of his car, before interrupting himself: 'Well, the important thing is that you're okay.'

Rob and I phoned our insurance companies, and then stood on the street outside a hole-in-the-wall pizza joint. He was twenty-three years old and on his way home to Newcastle. The Commodore belonged to his parents.

'It's only the run-around car,' he told me.

'It doesn't matter! A car is a car!' I said, glancing at his vehicle and then at Brad's scrunched VW.

After an hour it began to drizzle. We walked around the corner to the police station. When the sergeant realised he would have to write a report, he sighed, picked up a small black book and hauled himself to the counter.

We each made a statement. Rob used passive verbs ('I was hit from behind', not 'Kate hit me from behind'). Before I gave my statement, which would match Rob's account, I asked the officer, whose age I couldn't guess because the starchy blue uniform clouded any accurate assessment – twenty? Fifty? – if I could first phone a towing company. I'd pay outright for the tow to Newcastle.

'I've already inconvenienced Rob so much, and I want to get him home as soon as possible,' I said.

My request had the unintended effect of disarming the policeman's brusqueness. He asked if he could do anything to help.

'Could you recommend a tow truck company?' I asked.

'I'm not allowed to. There was a time when corrupt police used to be in bed with the tow truckers.'

'Right. Of course.'

I rang a local place and got a quote for $550.

Then I made my statement. It was a legal confession.

'I feel awful,' I told the officer. 'What if a pedestrian had been walking between our cars?'

'It could happen to anyone,' he assured me. 'It is part of living in Sydney. I'll be travelling on the M5 later today, and it could happen to me.'

In trying to make me feel better, he had erased human agency, as if *our* crashing into somebody happens *to* us. Then he said, almost reluctantly, that he'd have to write me a $311 ticket for negligent driving.

'Expect it in the post,' he said.

Negligent driving? It sounded serious.

'It's not a criminal offence, is it?'

'No, no. It's a traffic offence. You'll have a traffic offence record, not a criminal record.'

He gave me his card and told me to ring him if I needed to.

Rob and I walked back to our cars. His parents had decided to have the car towed to a garage in Sydney. I had to go. I paid for the tow, and gave Rob all the cash in my wallet for a taxi to the station and a train ticket home. Brad had collected Jemima and was waiting for me so he could return to the office.

When I arrived home and began sobbing, Brad made a valiant effort to console me before hurrying back to work.

A couple of hours later, I rang Rob. Yes, he had caught the train okay.

I wanted to tell him that I'd accidentally rear-ended him because I'd been distracted by the dozens of court matters stuck to me like glue. I wanted to say that in court, people's accounts of disgrace and misery flew at me and clung to my skin, invading my mouth, nose and ears.

I wanted to call my father and tell him that his daughter could no longer bear the tiny traces of his past, the way they left me guessing about him and us, and that it was time he told me something about his early life.

And I wanted to call Brad and say that those slights of his couldn't be brushed aside; that, if we were to go on, they had to be collected and named and dealt with; and that, if Freud were here, he would say that my crashing the VW was no accident.

All these raw happenings, sticky and swarming in the way of insects, hadn't accrued sufficient bulk for me to make sense of them – or perhaps it would be in the 'making-sense-of' that they might build mass. I had to give them narrative weight so that they might succumb to gravitation and finally be pushed off and freed from me forever.

Instead, I hung up the phone from Rob and sat in our green armchair sipping strong, sweet tea, while Jemima built Lego towers at my feet.

11

After the crash, I avoided the courts for a week, and instead absorbed myself in judges' sentencing.

I read about a 21-year-old man who had attacked a guy at a pub in Albury in country New South Wales. He'd left the poor victim with injuries so severe that the fellow's left eye had to be removed. The whole question of the offender's remorse caused a kerfuffle in the appeals court. It was all because the man had failed to tell the court how sorry he was.

The offender had been drunk at his local pub when he'd grabbed a young woman's backside. The woman's male friend, who had not been drinking, told the man not to touch her. The man spat at the woman's friend, who spat back. When the friend turned to leave, he felt something smash his face. The glass shattered and he saw only blackness as the man continued to hit him until security intervened.

In court the offender pleaded guilty to recklessly inflicting grievous bodily harm. His lawyer argued he was remorseful, presenting to the court reports from a forensic psychiatrist and a counsellor, as well as references from the offender's family and friends. People wrote of his shame, of his 'deep feelings of despair and regret', and of his 'genuine remorse'. On the day of the man's sentencing, the judge read out his judgment. He took into account the offender's youth, that he had no criminal record, and that he was being imprisoned for the first time; however, the judge was unconvinced of the depth of contrition: 'I would have liked to have seen more in the way of concern' for the victim, and the man's remorse 'might have been more forthcoming'. He sentenced him to four and a half years in prison, with a non-parole period of three years.

The reason why the judge was unconvinced of the offender's remorse was because the man never gave verbal evidence of it in court. The judge never heard from him. The offender appealed the length of the jail sentence, arguing that the judge had 'erred' when assessing his remorse, for wasn't he entitled to rely solely on psychologists' reports and family references? Confusion arose in the NSW Court of Criminal Appeal as to whether or not an offender who is making a submission of remorse is required, by law, to give sworn evidence. Must judges hear it from horses' mouths?

The appeals court dismissed the offender's application. The man's jail term would remain as it was. But in an act of dexterous legal manoeuvring, the court managed to declare two seemingly competing findings: first, that 'there is no statutory requirement that an offender give evidence before remorse can be taken into account in the calculation of sentence'; and, second, 'in assessing the weight of evidence of remorse [the judge was] entitled to take into the account the fact that the [offender] did not give evidence'.

In other words, in order to argue you are remorseful, you're not legally obliged to get into the witness box and speak of your remorse, but you are probably disadvantaged if you don't.

*

Two weeks after the car accident, when I still hadn't received a fine in the mail, I tentatively suggested to Brad that the police sergeant had taken into account my sincere remorse and had chosen not to record the conviction.

'Are you *kidding*?' he said. 'The ticket will come. Just you wait.'

One afternoon at uni, I received a call on my mobile from someone called Wayne. He was Rob's father. In the seventeen days since the accident, I'd assumed that all was being taken care of via my insurance company. Brad's car had been fixed, and I assumed Rob's family's car had too.

'It's not been that straightforward for us,' Wayne told me.

I crouched on the asphalt for better reception and listened as he sketched out the story of the past fortnight. He told me that his car was never comprehensively insured and that my insurance company had assessed the damage and decided that the car was not worth fixing. The car had been deemed a write-off even though it was fixable ('It's worth five or six thousand to our family'); Wayne and his wife had not taken out comprehensive insurance because Rob was under twenty-five years of age and the cost would have been too high; now the car was waiting in a smash repairs shop in Kingsford, and if it wasn't towed away tomorrow, it would cost Wayne $50 a day to keep it there. Wayne had arranged a tow truck to collect it and wanted the guy to make him an offer on the spare parts.

I wondered why Wayne had phoned me, and then it came: he needed me to go to Kingsford and collect the number plates from his car. He was worried that the plates might get stolen and used in a robbery. And there were months left on the registration and he wanted to return the plates to the Roads & Traffic Authority and receive a partial refund.

'Some belongings have already been stolen from the car,' Wayne added.

We had an elliptical conversation. I deduced, wrongly, that the insurance company wouldn't give him what the car was worth pre-accident.

'So you've essentially lost a car?' I asked.

'Yes,' he told me.

I had to go. I was late collecting Jemima. I'd call him that night. *Somehow I must find and give Wayne's family $5000 for a car*, I decided. I took a stab at my tax return estimate, and figured I could scrape together additional funds. *This is what it is to take responsibility*, I kept saying to myself. *This is what is required. It was your fault. Own it.*

At home Brad was furious.

'You've done everything right. You stayed with Rob at the accident scene. You paid for the tow. You gave Rob money to get home! Most people, when they have a car accident, just swap details and say, "My insurance will handle it," and they don't ever have to speak to one another again. This guy is *calling* you? I'd call the insurance company and tell them you're being harassed. You *cannot* go and get those number plates and send them up to Newcastle. What signal does that send? Next thing they're going to ask you for a new car!'

'But I'm responsible,' I told him.

'You've taken responsibility by being insured. Our cars are insured! That's the point of responsibility. You and I have already done the responsible thing. What if the "getting the number plates" story is just a way to lure you to a smash repairs shop before you're assaulted or kidnapped or something?'

'I told Wayne I'd do it. I have to keep my word.'

'For*get* about your word.'

I phoned Wayne. Wasn't the insurance company paying him the value of the car pre-accident?

'Yes,' he said. 'But it's not that straightforward.'

Why wasn't it straightforward?

Brad mimed: *Get off the phone*. Wayne thanked me for agreeing to collect the number plates and told me that his wife would call me in the morning with the details. I hung up.

'You cannot go and get those number plates. You cannot,' Brad resumed.

'Shhh. You'll wake up Jemima. Don't get so worked up.'

He calmed, taking my hand: 'I just feel you're being manipulated.'

In our conversations, I had told Wayne I was sorry. I'd rear-ended a car in traffic. I didn't know how many more times I could say sorry or what exactly I was supposed to do. Surely I couldn't just arrive at the smash repairs and ask for number plates? And what if I packaged them, sent them off and they went missing?

In what felt like a betrayal of Wayne, I phoned my insurance company. A nice young woman reassured me that Wayne would receive market value for the car plus payment for scrapping. She told me *not* to go and get the number plates, that it was something Wayne should arrange with the scrapper. She would call Wayne right now and explain everything to him and make sure it would all be okay.

'Do *not* buy him a new car,' she told me. 'We process a thousand claims a day. Accidents happen.'

The next morning Wayne's wife didn't phone me. I didn't collect the plates.

Three weeks later the traffic fine arrived in the post.

12

Lately I had begun to wonder if a judge's experience of sentencing people was a sort of high-stakes form of tertiary marking. At our university we used grading rubrics, assessing university essays against stated criteria. A student's mark was not spat out based on grids, nor was it plucked from the air. Rather, we lecturers had folded the department's marking 'rules' into our intellectual practice, which meant that our grading process was a feeling thing. We could sense where an assignment sat. The same piece of work would be marked by two or three different teachers and we would mostly arrive at the same result.

I'd been interviewing judges for more than a year, asking them how they assessed a person's remorse. Until recently, I'd been disinclined to directly address with them the practice of sentencing because I thought I already knew the answer: law and criminology scholarship referred to a judge's process as one of 'intuitive synthesis'. The expression is used to describe the way in which a judge considers the penalty range of an offence together with a mass of subjective information to settle on a sentence. For instance, two men might commit an armed robbery at a convenience store. Superficially it would seem that both men should receive the same sentence; however, the older man has a long criminal record and a history of violence, while the younger man has no criminal record, was coopted into the offence, confessed to the police, expressed remorse and assisted in apprehending his accomplice. In arriving at the two sentences, a judge must also consider the 'objective seriousness' of the offence. Were guns, knives, baseball bats or syringes used? How much cash was stolen? What property was taken? Was the victim threatened, beaten or shot? Judges and magistrates draw on their deep knowledge of case law, and their experience of people, to arrive at a sentence that sits in an appropriate range.

I liked the common-sense sound of the term 'intuitive synthesis'. In flicking it around in my mind, I felt I'd grasped the judiciary's work. However, a clumsy, last-minute question to a magistrate changed that.

I had visited the NSW Coroner's Court in Glebe, a short, flat building that stretches for a third of a block on Parramatta Road, and had sat with Magistrate Hugh Dillon in his office that looked out to a foliage-filled courtyard. Dillon, a reflective, softly spoken fellow with the hands of a violinist, was a public prosecutor until he became a magistrate in 1996, and in 2008 he was appointed deputy state coroner. The day we met he wore thin, purple-rimmed glasses and a gold necktie speckled with music notes.

Before he began presiding over inquests into deaths – witnessing doctors confront grieving families whose babies have died; consoling widows of traumatised policemen who had taken their own lives – Dillon worked in the court sentencing people. He told me that remorse is the most critical element in the criminal law because it reduces the pain for the victim and it enables the community to reintegrate the offender; that the impact of remorse 'is far greater if it comes from the horse's mouth' than if it comes mediated through a lawyer; that judges and coroners have 'tremendous advantage' over magistrates because sometimes they actually get to hear from the offenders themselves, thereby 'connecting corporeally with them'; and that the Local Court system is 'a bit like a sausage factory', where magistrates process dozens of matters each day and where time constraints usually make it impossible for offenders to give sworn evidence. We also spoke about his role as a coroner, the weightiness of it, how he had to ensure that deaths, and suspected deaths, were properly investigated. He told me that, at the end of inquests, he tried to speak in court in such a way as to offer some solace to distressed loved ones.

'It's priest-like,' I said, to which he replied: 'I almost became a priest. In my twenties I was a Jesuit novice.'

It was probably my feeling so at ease with Hugh ('Call me Hugh,' he'd insisted) that prompted me to blurt out the question: 'What am I not asking that I should be asking? What questions should I be asking judges? What should I be asking them that I haven't so far asked you?'

Hugh was silent. When he began speaking, I entered a stunned state.

'I would like to know from judges how they really arrive at a sentence,' he said. 'We have all this stuff we have to take into account. What's the objective seriousness of the offence? We are supposed to look at it on a spectrum of "most serious of all" to "least serious of all", and somehow we tootle along the piano keys and try to say where it fits on that spectrum. Then we say, "Okay, that's our starting point," and then that's complicated by "standard non-parole periods", which is another bullshit thing. And we have Section 21A, which has all sorts of things that sound like someone's been playing chess with someone else who's got countermoves. And then we go back to basic principles – deterrence, rehabilitation, punishment, general deterrence. We say things that we actually don't do. We say, "Okay, we've got to take into account general deterrence. We've got to tell the community this is a bad thing. We've got to denounce it." Does anyone in the community not know that stealing is a bad thing?'

I didn't know what to say.

'Doesn't "intuitive synthesis" reflect the judge's experience of sentencing someone?' I finally asked.

'Yes, but what does that actually mean?' he said. 'I don't pretend to speak for all magistrates or judges or our courts, but I think that the process is unnecessarily complex and intellectually turgid, overladen with all sorts of rules and guidelines. Sentencing has become an abstract, Byzantine dance of words. It's Hermann Hesse's *The Glass Bead Game*.'

Having not studied law, nor Hesse's novel, I understood neither part of Hugh's analogy.

I borrowed *The Glass Bead Game* from the library, a thick, crazy sort of book about intellectuals who play the glass bead game, the rules of which are elusive. Set centuries into the future in a fictional European province, Castalia, citizens strive to master the game that is based on conceptual connections between seemingly unrelated topics. Invented by a musicologist, the game requires deep knowledge of music, maths and history. Players perform an abstract fusion of all arts and sciences, but the rules are never made clear and the exercise makes little sense.

I kept reading. I clambered my way through scholarly law articles, and through 'question papers' on sentencing released by the NSW Law Reform Commission. At first the material felt impenetrable. But after a while, in small lumps and trickles, the information assimilated itself into my cognition, and I understood what Hugh meant.

For judges and magistrates in the NSW criminal justice system, the number of prescribed matters they must take into account when sentencing someone, and the accompanying algorithms applying to discounts and aggravation, had grown so vast that the process had become worryingly esoteric. Since the 1980s, successive NSW state governments had introduced legislation curbing judicial discretion. It was the result of a 'law and order auction', as critics put it, as governments and oppositions vied for the tougher-party-on-crime mantle. In the late 1990s, the government introduced 'guideline judgments': model cases that reflected a sentencing scale in commonly encountered situations. Judges were told that if they departed from the guideline case when arriving at a sentence they were required to give a reason. In 2002, 'standard non-parole periods' for some offences were introduced (40 per cent of the maximum sentence for some offences, 80 per cent for others), and a mandate to judicial officers that, should they wish to depart from these standard minimums, they were required to give one or more reasons drawn from a formal list.

There were also 'sentencing discounts', where offenders were eligible for a reduced sentence if they pleaded guilty at an early stage, and a further discount if they assisted police. The thinking was that guilty pleas saved the court time and money, and saved victims from having to give evidence. An offender who pleaded guilty before being committed to trial was eligible for a 25 per cent reduction; an offender who pleaded guilty after committal got up to 12.5 per cent off.

The government's rationale was that the legislation would achieve greater consistency in the sentencing process, and render it more transparent to the public. It wasn't clear either goal had been achieved. Meanwhile, the changes had increased the actual labour of judicial officers, who had to write more and more elaborate, often mind-boggling judgments if they were to withstand the scrutiny of the appeals courts.

I phoned Hugh.

'If sentencing is like this now, what did it used to be like?' I asked.

'When I first went into practice, we used to talk about the "tariff",' he said. 'The "tariff" was the range within which a particular offence would fall. In a drug importation case, for example, everyone understood that a certain amount of heroin imported by a courier with no previous criminal history in Australia would attract a tariff of three to five years' jail. Judges could work out the exact sentence by going up and down the scale between three and five years depending on the subjective factors, but they would stay within that range. A sentence hearing in the District or Supreme Court might last an hour. These days it might last three or four.'

The problem, he explained, was that current processes did not suit this 'synthesised' approach but instead implicitly encouraged a sort of phoney science.

'Some judges try to place a mathematical range on the kinds of discounts that offenders receive,' he said. 'When sentencing a person, they sit there and think, *Okay, this sentence ought to be four years*, and then they turn to a formal list of aggravating and mitigating factors, and add and subtract all these little bits and pieces before arriving at three years and eight months – *Okay, I've not only got to give him a discount for the early plea, but I've got to nominate a number. He pleaded guilty a month after being charged, so I might give him fifteen per cent. What's fifteen per cent off three years and eight months?* – and they go and work that out on an abacus or something. It's fake mathematics because not only are there no set numbers for these factors, but the original starting point is discretionary. One judge might have had the original number as four and a half years, while another might have three and a half.'

I sought out more judges. I phoned Andrew Haesler, a NSW District Court judge whom I'd met the previous year at a symposium on 'Neuroscience and Law' during which he'd been a guest speaker.

'You can have logical, coherent sentencing with some mathematical elements, but too much maths skews the process,' he told me. 'If we want robots to sentence people, then employ robots. But it won't be fair, and it won't be just.'

Haesler said that even those judges who tried to adopt an intuitive synthesis approach now also kept a calculator on their desks. One judge had 'Intuitive Synthesiser' written on his calculator.

I spoke with another District Court judge who described the legislation as 'a matrix, a labyrinth that you've got to work your way through', and a former magistrate who told me that this intense labour did not result in a better sentence; it was simply that judges must undertake this process if they did not want their decisions overturned on appeal. The then NSW attorney-general, a former public prosecutor, recognised what he called the 'ridiculous complexity' of NSW sentencing legislation, and had ordered the NSW Law Reform Commission to review the *Sentencing Act*. In the years to come, the Act would be amended, with standard non-parole periods no longer having a determinative significance, and instead simply being 'a matter to be taken into account by a court in determining the appropriate sentence'.

The sentencing legislation was enacted partly in response to community perceptions, beaten up by radio shock jocks and the rest of the tabloid media, that sentences were too lenient and disparate. The thing was, however, most judges and magistrates arrived at sentences within a similar range. Those who imposed unduly lenient or astonishingly punitive sentences left themselves open to having their decisions overturned on appeal. As for soft sentencing, such as non-custodial and community-based sentences, research indicated that when members of the public were given material relevant to a case – information about sentencing, an account of the case facts, the circumstances of the offender, a statement from the victim – people's desire to punish dropped dramatically and they often settled on more lenient sentences than a judge would have imposed.

At stake in all this, I realised, was the idea of wisdom: what we think it is, and what we want it to do. I'd want a wise person to sit in judgment on me, someone with experience, intellectual honesty, ethics and compassion. But these complex sentencing procedures in NSW inhibited the wisdom of judges. They impeded the very quality we need most in our courts: the capacity of judges to gently weigh the unquantifiable circumstances of wrongdoing, broken lives and that most ungraspable of things – the human soul – so that they might reach just decisions.

13

Each year at the beginning of summer when I was little, my father assessed Year 12 mathematics exams. He would arrive home with cardboard boxes filled with two thousand Higher School Certificate booklets, lugging them down our hallway, stacking them in the dining room. This task was not part of his academic job. He took it on because the pay was good, the extra money coming in handy for Christmas and New Year expenses. Dad was part of a marking team, each team being assigned to a different maths question, and a weekend was spent together getting the marking scale embedded, so each marker marked uniformly.

It was December and the cedar table in our dining room exuded a warm, woody smell. Dad had bought it for a bargain and then restored it. It was his hobby, rescuing tables, chairs, bookcases and chests of drawers from used furniture shops. He detested hoarding, and only purchased what was needed, bringing the pieces home, lovingly sanding them, varnishing them, then safeguarding them from crayons and sticky fingers. I envied the physical care he showed these objects.

During exam season he sat at the cedar table on weekends, head bent, brow creased. I would tiptoe in and pull up a chair, fascinated by the marvellous hieroglyphics that absorbed him. Years later, when my siblings and I were older, mathematics became a point of intersection in our household. It was a language all five of us were willing to speak together. Occasionally at dinner we would talk intimately about an equation or an algorithm, or we'd play card games. During those evenings, the messiness of human exchange dissolved – past, present and future was suspended – for all that existed was sublime numerical relationship.

But at the time of the exam papers, I did not yet have a handle on the elaborate patterns. Dad would open a booklet, carefully scan the student's workings-out, and write a number at the bottom. He'd turn the page and do the same. Then again. Each student had completed, or had attempted to complete, three or four problems, which meant that Dad had to tally the three or four scores in order to reach the overall grade. I helped him: 3 + 2 + 2 + 1. Eight! He'd record the mark on the front of the booklet. Sometimes he wrote '0' and I was crestfallen at the blunt summation of the student's performance; but sometimes he wrote '10' and murmured 'Well done' to the young person who would never hear it.

The steps of the process seemed so clean: Dad's pen forming impressions on the page, the crisp addition of numbers. A perfect dance between assessor and assessed. Watching him examine the work, I stepped into the slipstream of his thoughts, as if the calculus had sacred access to my father that was unavailable to me, but if I sat close enough to the alchemy I could slide in unnoticed.

*

The memory of my father and the exam papers came to me one Thursday. I was driving up the coast of New South Wales to speak with a magistrate who ran a courthouse in a small town. The bush was thick around these parts, it provided a pleasing canopy, and the highway felt like a winding tunnel.

The forest on the side of the road gave way to dwellings. Around a bend was the town's welcome sign and, a little further on, the nineteenth-century courthouse building. I parked directly out front and slipped inside.

The courtroom was a sweet, narrow box-shaped space painted pink, cream and federation green. With its lofty ceiling and wooden detail, I imagined it might feature in a period drama. I bowed towards the bench, and sat at the back of the public gallery.

Proceedings were underway. The magistrate dispensed with her paperwork from the previous case, and announced the next matter. It concerned a man called Mr Moore.

Moore stood, tight-jawed. A few months ago he had been stopped by police, in the early evening, driving out of the underground car park at the local Coles supermarket. He was breathalysed. The police had been tipped off. They knew where he'd be and they knew he'd be drunk. Moore pleaded guilty to 'mid-range drink-driving' and 'driving while disqualified'.

The magistrate stared at him: 'Your behaviour presents an unacceptable risk to other people.' She said that his driving record was 'appalling', that this was the seventh time he'd been before the court for drink-driving. She must impose a term of imprisonment, she said.

Moore looked lost. He was older than me, a decade maybe, and there was something of a white-goods store manager about him. It was that suit, that neck. His lawyer asked the magistrate to consider an intensive corrections order, a new sentencing option that included home detention, curfews, random drug-and-alcohol screens, community service and rehabilitation. Moore had kids. He didn't want to lose access to them.

On the magistrate's face was a flicker of relief. She didn't *want* to send him to jail. She disqualified him from holding a licence for two years before adjourning the matter so that Mr Moore could be assessed as to his eligibility for an intensive corrections order. The magistrate stood. We stood. She exited.

A court officer led me around the back of the building to the office. Having interviewed Supreme Court judges in city skyscrapers, I expected Her Honour's chambers to be lined with spacious bookshelves, but instead she sat at an ordinary desk in a poky room with tired carpet. You got the sense that, in the rainy season, it became mildewy.

She greeted me all smiles and handshakes, threw off her black judicial robe, and hung it up. She asked me if I'd had lunch. I had. Someone knocked on her door and put a plate of hot chips on her desk.

'You don't mind if I eat?' she asked.

'Of course not,' I said.

As she took a chip, I studied her. She was in her fifties and had the sort of balanced face you see on people such as artists or doctors who might know something of the human condition. She'd not been on the bench for long, she told me. For the first two years, she came to court every day feeling like throwing up.

'The job's very fast,' she explained. 'I might see one hundred matters a day, and sentence twenty or thirty people. The law is cut-throat. If you're not in control of the court, the lawyers will smell blood and they'll be running it. They'll be running *you*. I've got to at least *look* like I know what I'm doing – and, at the same time, I'm learning on the job. A lot of it is about actual court craft skills, managing and running the court where you've got lots of stressed people in front of you. This morning I noticed a woman in the gallery who looked as if she was having a panic attack, so I interrupted proceedings and told her to see the nurse. Also, being the only magistrate in town adds to the pressure because there's no one else to get through things. One day I had a shocking case of conjunctivitis. My eyes blew up and I had to go into court facing ninety people.'

She began to calculate Mr Moore's sentence. She took a piece of paper from a neat stack at the corner of her desk. It was a form she'd created to help her sentence people at speed. She showed me where she would jot down bald facts, and where she'd scribble in boxes, noting the 'aggravating' factors of Moore's case, any 'mitigating' factors, and 'subjective' details about him. At the bottom of the page were listed the seven official purposes of sentencing such as 'to ensure that the offender is adequately punished for the offence'; and 'to make the offender accountable for his or her actions'.

'The sentencing process is extraordinarily complicated. I think of it as a puzzle,' she told me. 'I've got to make sure I have all the pieces, and that all the pieces are together. If you leave out a piece, your sentence will be appealed. Then I have to arrive at a decision. It's a huge task.'

She worried about her own inconsistency – which is why she had drawn up this form. She also worried about consistency between judges.

'We judges have our own philosophies,' she said. 'For instance, I like Buddhism. This job gives me all day, every day, the opportunity to exercise compassion.'

An office person knocked: 'Sorry to interrupt,' she said. 'Admin asked me to ask you did you want the microwave – the old microwave – because we're getting a new one.'

'Do I want the microwave?' replied the magistrate. 'No. Thanks.'

'No?' the woman said. 'Alright.' She left.

The magistrate nibbled another chip. She asked me if I'd seen the Judicial Information Research System. I hadn't.

'Pull up a chair,' she said.

I sat close, our forearms almost touching, and studied her computer screen. The system, she told me, contained case law, legislation, principles of sentencing, sentencing statistics and other information.

'Let's say I've got Mr Moore, mid-range Prescribed Concentration of Alcohol,' she said. 'He's under the *Road Transport Act*, so I look at the offence he's charged under.'

She wiped her oily fingers before using the mouse to click on a drop-down box.

'I look at the Local Court statistics. Here are all the sentences in NSW from January 2008. Since then, a total of 41,600 people have been sentenced for mid-range drink-driving.'

She continued: 'But I'm thinking, *Hang on a minute. What about my guy?* Well, who *is* my guy? I go to "Offender Type" —'

She clicked on another drop-down box.

'My guy's got two offences. Okay, there's 8000 people.'

Another box.

'My guy has a prior record of the same type. Okay, there's 4500 of them.'

Another click.

'My guy's entered a plea of guilty, so we're building in his discount. There's 2600 of them.'

Click.

'Mr Moore is aged between forty-one and fifty. That brings it down to 390 people.'

On the screen were columns – a bell curve – indicating how many of those 390 people received what sort of sentence: No recorded conviction? Suspended sentence? Good behaviour bond? Community service? Home detention? Jail?

She said: 'I'm thinking, *Well, only two people got no recorded conviction. I can't give him that. I'd get appealed. And only twelve went to jail.* This is what I do in my head. I immediately go from the bottom to the top.'

She began by pointing to the lightest sentence and working up.

'I think, *That's four, eight, nine, ten, fourteen to seventeen per cent. So eighty-three per cent of people got between a fine and a community service order*. I might write that on a little sticker. I'm getting a range here now. And I'm thinking, *Well how bad was my guy?* I'm not just going to fine him and disqualify his licence; this is his eighth time, so he's going to be upwards towards this end,' she said, pointing to the jail column.

Then she took a breath, pushing her chair away from the desk, away from the computer and the form and the numbers.

'In the end,' she said slowly, 'the sentence I come up with will be the sentence that feels right.'

We talked of country life, of sentencing laws, and of sagacity. I thanked her, we said goodbye and I drove south.

One month later, the magistrate and Mr Moore would meet in the quaint box courtroom. She'd ask him to stand as she read out her judgment. He would hear his lot, a punishment decided on messy legislation, statistics, puzzle sheets, bell curves, button-clicks, calculators, the tabloid press, politics, philosophy, the history of God, the history of science, and on one woman's visceral certainty that justice has been delivered.

III

PRISON AND PAROLE

14

Ethnography is, or can feel like, a sort of spying. For all their best intentions, ethnographers know that the phrase 'spend time with people' is a euphemism for 'infiltrate'. You are welcomed into hidden worlds, received into private spaces. You amass reams of field notes written with painstaking detail and distance. You write from doorways, from the edges of goings-on.

So much watching and listening.

When I was five, the threadbare carpet in our family home was removed and replaced with flecked-cream wool pile. We had just returned to Sydney from a year of living in Oxford where my father was a visiting researcher. The Oxford house we rented belonged to a significant person, my parents had been told, although no one knew who it was. It wasn't until the release of information under the *Official Secrets Act* many years later that they discovered the owner had been Jack Good. Good was a genius statistician and had been central to wartime intelligence, being one of the Bletchley Park code breakers who had worked with Alan Turing.

During the English winter, I had come to know snow, delighting in the way it cradled my figure when I lay on my back in the icy garden. Back in Sydney, when our new carpet was installed, I stretched out on the floor and tried to make angel shapes by running my arms across the fibres.

Mum loved that carpet. It hid dust, she said. I loved it too. It was cushiony underfoot and allowed for creeping. Whenever my father was home, I would glide through the rooms, peek through doorways, locate him, and then spend the days monitoring the distance between us both. It was a means of avoiding those arrows of blame he aimed at us kids. The house was compact: a three-bedroom cottage built in 1907 by an auctioneer and therefore not in the grand style that was the fashion. My parents had bought the place before they'd had children. It had needed repairs. The back section, once an open verandah but since closed in, was falling apart. In the kitchen were remnants of a wood-fire stove. The floor was covered with thin, ratty carpet through which you could see the rotting floorboards, and it was impossible to keep clean. The floor was also unstable. Before new boards were laid down, my parents had to execute a hopscotch routine to securely reach the bathroom, a manoeuvre made more difficult twelve months later when Mum was heavily pregnant with me. Mum's uncle was a builder. He mended the place structurally and slapped on wallpaper that had on it wild 1970s patterns, while Dad scraped and painted. By the time I was born, the little family had a solid home.

With the carpet in place, I moved ghost-like between the kitchen, the lounge room and the bedroom I shared with my sister. I practised the neat trick of splitting myself: one half absorbed in a book or in pipe-cleaner craft, the other watching and listening for the large male figure. My siblings had tricks of their own: she would sleep, those daytime naps a disappearing act; he would escape into an imaginative world of play. I preferred the splitting, for it seemed the most effective.

When a person repeats an action often enough, her body adapts, and eventually by adulthood I had become two people: the alert woman, her face perpetually turned towards the world; and the remote, hidden one putting pen to paper.

*

Jemima was almost four years old. In the evenings we had baths together, flopping flannels on our faces and fronts, washing away the day. We'd study one another's bodies: the freckle on her left arm, my squishy bellybutton, the shampoo in her hair a halo of suds. She'd swivel around and fold herself into me, our bodies loosening together, and I'd cradle her, kissing her milky shoulders, marvelling at the reduction of things. In these moments we were not 'her and me' but a combined form, perfect in, and made perfect by, the water.

When she was two, sometimes we had shared showers. We got 'nudie rudie' and I hugged her tight, gently twisting my torso so that the warm stream spilled down her soft little back and sides. One time she'd been in no mood to wash. I should've given her a quick wipe down. Instead, I clutched the kicking creature to me. She was slippery to hold, so I sat her on the tiles. She plucked every item from the shower recess – a plastic cup, a toy submarine, a nailbrush, the soap, the shampoo – and hurled them across the bathroom. With nothing left to throw, she screamed and cried and smacked me on my naked backside.

Jemima's tantrums had produced in me an internal splintering; we were not a single organism, nor was she a cute extension of me. She was alien.

Now that Jemima was older, whenever she lost her temper, we would coach her to apologise. Occasionally there were floods of contrite tears, but mostly her regret sounded robotic.

'Daddy isn't my friend anymore,' she told me. 'He won't take me to the playground.'

'He took you to the playground yesterday. He's busy today. If you feel upset, you need to talk to him about it. You can't just hit him. You hit Daddy. That's not okay. I know you felt very mad, and it's okay to feel mad, but we don't go around hitting people. You need to say "Sorry" to him.'

Protracted staring at the floor.

'Go on. Off you go, sweetheart. Go to him and say, "Sorry, Dad, for hitting you. I won't do it again."'

Slinking over to Daddy.

'Are you wanting to say something to me?' asked Brad.

More floor staring.

'Sorry,' she mumbled.

'Sorry for what?'

'SorryforhittingyouIwontdoitagain.'

She was little, but the perfunctoriness of the declaration irked me, for it was my conviction that people must take responsibility for what they do; they must apologise properly. *Say it like you mean it*, I wanted to tell her, even while I knew that children do not possess the full capacity for remorse.

A judge had talked to me about the principle of *doli incapax*: incapable of crime. Children under ten cannot be held legally responsible for their actions and therefore cannot be convicted of committing a criminal offence; if the child is aged ten to fourteen, the state has to prove she knew her actions were seriously wrong and not simply naughty. Apparently it has to do with the biological development of young people: the part of our brain we supposedly use to exercise good judgment, to self-reflect, to empathise, doesn't reach maturation until we are twenty-five years old. A friend told me that her perspective on punishment changed when her son became a teenager. He had scaled a fence and fell, almost snapping his neck. 'Every judge should have a teenage son,' she said. 'Teenage boys are daft and do mad things. They don't think. They have no impulse control.'

Remorse is a cognitive skill. It has to be learnt.

Recently I had phoned a prisoner rights organisation and had been put in touch with a former inmate. The fifty-year-old man had spent fifteen months in Long Bay jail. During his incarceration, he'd been a mentor to the other prisoners. He'd noticed how frightened and poorly educated they were; boys full of bravado, with low self-esteem, unable to express themselves. When the young men were up for parole, they would try to show the appearance of remorse. Some were convincing actors. They would even cry. 'But members of the parole board know human nature,' the man told me, 'and they could see through it.' He told his fellow inmates: 'After the parole people have asked you a few questions about the nature of your remorse, they'll be able to see that you don't really feel it. In order to show remorse, you've got to feel genuine remorse.'

In jail, he wrote a pamphlet – *How to Feel Genuine Remorse* – which he circulated to the other prisoners. He emailed me a copy. He'd composed a section, 'Be Truly Remorseful', which he'd identified as the most important part of both the parole and rehabilitation process: 'accept what you've done by not denying what happened that put you in here'; 'accept what you did was wrong'; 'take responsibility for your actions'; 'recognise the bad effect your actions have had on the victim and show remorse for what a victim is going through'. An image of a twisted acting class came to me: a bunch of tattooed blokes in the prison yard wandering around, clutching this document and saying to themselves: 'I've got to feel it to show it. I've got to feel it to show it.'

One night Jemima and I dried ourselves after a bath. I dressed her in pyjamas and she scuttled off to play. I cleared away dinner.

When I peeked into her room I found her sitting at the centre of a moat of shreddings. She was using the clunky scissors to cut paper. Seeing me watching her, she went pink: 'Sorry, Mum. Sorry. I'm *so* sorry. I *was* being careful.' I gave her a remonstrating look and then cuddled her. She handed me the sharp instrument and we tidied away the mess. I read her a Hairy Maclary book, and put her to bed.

Brad was due home soon. I sat on the sofa with a cup of tea and looked out at the dark shapes of the trees.

In other circumstances, Jemima would have tried to conceal the scissors. Had our wooden floors heralded my approach, she would have whipped them behind her back, but I was wearing thick wool socks, a silent padding. I'd inadvertently caught her in the act.

The recollection and its corollary were swift: when I was growing up, the carpet in my parents' house had muffled my footsteps, but it had also masked my father's. Who knew when he might enter a room and catch you out? I second-guessed myself, watching my movements and reading them for mischief or misjudgment, continually exposed to my own hyper-vigilant gaze. This might have been Dad's experience as a little boy at that hostel: the forced internalisation of a second-person catechism:

Have you spilt a drop of milk?

Are your shoes scuffed? Have you shined them?

Are you speaking too loud, or too soft?

My father also learnt this self-surveillance from his mother. She had worked in radio in the late 1940s in Vienna. The airwaves were strictly controlled, which meant she adhered to a script. A Soviet soldier would sit in the room with my grandmother, pointing a loaded rifle at her, following her every word lest she trip up.

As a child, despite the self-attentiveness, you cannot ever be certain you're not getting things wrong. My strategy was always to cloak myself in contrition. Children may not have developed the full capacity for remorse, but they learn early of its power. I'd inhabited it like a cocoon. I was now almost forty years old, but one doesn't easily shake off one's chrysalis. I did not know whether I needed to purge myself of remorse, or if it needed to purge itself of me.

If you critique every act you have carried out and might carry out, you need a system that forensically teases apart people's sayings and doings in order to find bona fide mistakes. It was why I'd turned up at that woman's sentencing two and a half years ago. It was why since then I'd observed case after case. To watch means you can see what has really happened, who has done what to whom, and who must say sorry.

*

Brad turned forty.

We dropped off Jemima at his parents', took a taxi to the airport and flew to Tasmania. We hired a car in Hobart and drove ninety minutes up the east coast to a house on a headland overlooking Great Oyster Bay. We couldn't really afford this trip, but we couldn't afford not to take it either.

For three days we read, talked, ate, drank, laughed and held one another. We remembered why we were together.

An architect known for his modernist compositions had designed the place. It was all steel and glass. We could see the trail the convicts used two hundred years ago to trudge up from the beach below, and where, for thousands of years before European arrival, the Aboriginal Oyster Bay people harvested shellfish. From almost every angle we could see the horizon, imagining Antarctica just beyond it. We were awed by the soft light and the stillness of the bush, how the surroundings felt prehistoric, how we half-expected a long-extinct creature to slowly pad its way around the headland, making giant prints in the sand.

For three nights I slept. There was a dreamlessness. I thought, wrongly, that a healing had been reached.

15

The offices of the Parole Authority were in western Sydney. I began visiting them, driving out to Parramatta's Justice Precinct: a collection of glass-walled buildings and pathways that exuded happy order. The landscaped gardens included thick bushes of mint and lavender, clumps of chives and lemon trees. The original idea for Parramatta, devised in 1790, involved a grid system of five wide streets, a tick-tack-toe board of geometry and balance, and, while the city had since been overlaid by urban sprawl, traces of the plan remained. In the foyer of the Children's Court building was a sign: 'If you were here in 1804, you would be standing outside a small convict hut. Remains of the hut are still here!' At the centre of the place was the towering Sydney West Trial Courts building. The urban design pulled you to it.

On a Thursday at 9 am I attended a private meeting of the Parole Authority. I'd been attending them for weeks. Seven of us sat in a sunny boardroom that had an Aboriginal dot painting, a large, limp Australian flag and a detailed map of New South Wales sticky-taped to the wall. In total twenty people formed the Parole Authority: four judicial members, twelve community members and four 'official members' (representatives from Community Offender

Services NSW and the police force). But only five members sat at any given time, plus the secretary. Around the boardroom table that day were two university professors, a young, friendly parole officer whose writing was neat and fat like a primary school teacher's, a former undercover policeman with tattoos who once worked 'in the drug scene', and Ian Pike, chairman of the Authority. Pike, a former NSW chief magistrate, was a smart, compassionate man much liked by his peers. In his hometown Junee, a street had been named in his honour.

I had met Ian Pike eight weeks ago when I'd visited him at the NSW Judicial Commission where he worked two days a week.

'Remorse is very important for prisoners because, if they feel genuine remorse, they're more likely to address their offending behaviour and produce positive results during the various prison rehabilitation programs,' he'd told me.

I'd immediately warmed to Pike and his directness. He seemed to me rather elderly to be working the jobs he was. Months later he would tell me that he'd made some bad financial investments ('We Pikes have no luck with money'), the results of which had forced him out of retirement. But he also enjoyed what he did – and had reserves of energy with which to do it. Although he had the stoop, paunch and squint of a man well into his seventies, he still played squash.

It was Pike's idea that I sit in on private meetings, motivated as it was by his faith in public relations. He was concerned about how parole matters were reported in the press and that there was little clear, accurate information circulated to the public. He envisaged me writing a piece about the workings of the parole board – which indeed is what I ended up doing, my article published in a national magazine many months later.

In my mind, though, I was at those meetings to find out when precisely remorse comes upon you. Is it after you've been sentenced, when what you've done claws at you? Does it happen when you are sitting hour after hour, year after year, in a jail cell? Is that what the system meant by 'rehabilitation': thousands of people in cages experiencing slow-moving epiphanies?

I inspected the placemats on the boardroom table. They were calendars produced by the commercial arm of Corrective Services NSW. On them was written 'Quality Service. Quality People. Quality Products' alongside photos of prison guards chitchatting with jolly, green-clothed inmates.

At this meeting, as at all meetings, the Authority had to decide when to allow people to serve the remainder of their sentence in the community, as well as set the conditions of release. Unlike the work of the judiciary, with its baroque sentencing legislation, the job of the Authority was administrative. When people were given a custodial sentence, they usually received a non-parole period from a judge or magistrate, meaning that they were unable to apply for parole until a set date. If a person's sentence was less than three years, the court automatically issued a parole order; for sentences of three years or more, parole was decided by the Authority. Pike explained to me that parole was crucial as it was in the public interest to have offenders supervised in the community before their sentence expired. The Authority also had to decide whether or not to revoke parole when parole orders were breached.

Parole Authority members had in front of them their handwritten notes as well as a laptop with the files of inmates and parolees. The meeting got underway, and, before I knew it, they were leaping from one matter to the next. I scribbled snippets of conversation.

'He's still only young.'

'He made the big time early as a serious offender.'

The board made a parole order for an inmate.

'We'll use conditions four and seventeen.'

'Your four might be covered by eighteen.'

'So just leave it at fifteen and sixteen?'

'Yes.'

A parolee had tried to evade a mandatory urine test by substituting his own urine with a sample of animal pee. He somehow took it from his pet cat.

'At least he's not pregnant,' someone joked.

A parolee had died.

'It's immensely tragic.'

'The man overdosed in his bathroom. His fifteen-year-old daughter found him.' On his file they wrote 'Parolee Deceased'.

The board revoked a parolee's parole and issued a warrant for the man's arrest.

'I had A, B and D.'

'Me too.'

'I had A, B, D and K.'

'We don't need K.'

Pike turned to me: 'We use so many mnemonics, it's crazy.'

In front of me was a State Parole Authority booklet, which included lists with the corresponding numbers and letters that board members used to make decisions, but I couldn't keep up with their conversation. The secretary, however, could. She had twenty-three stamps on her desk and, like a bureaucratic pipe-organist, she listened to the voices around her while her hands opened, punched, closed and stacked files. Poking out the sides of each file were tags the colour of children's paints, and some files were so obese that the meagre manila folder was a bursting piece of skin.

The Authority made more than 10,000 decisions a year regarding inmates' parole. During each three-hour meeting, seventy matters were decided upon; on average, each matter was given less than three minutes of discussion. The rapid pace of parole meetings was made possible by board members reading their thick piles of documents in the days beforehand. For each inmate, members received the judge's sentencing remarks, a probation and parole report, and the inmate's criminal history. They might have also received medical reports, letters from the inmate's family or from the victim or victim's family, and, in the case of an offender who received a non-parole custodial sentence of twelve or more years, a report from the Serious Offenders Review Council.

As Authority members read the material at home, they made notes and recommendations, translating the mass of documents into a few letters and numbers. For example, a member might want to refuse the person's parole on the basis of 'C19' ('Needs to participate in a therapeutic program to address violence') and 'J46' ('Unconfirmed post-release accommodation'). Then at meetings they compared notes. Sometimes discussions were heated and a vote was taken. ('On the board there used to be a feminist medical doctor and a chauvinist high-school teacher and there was nearly blood on the floor,' one member told me.) But most often there was good-natured agreement. In fact, to me the process sounded like utopian Bingo ('I had fifteen, seventeen, eighteen, twenty-six.' 'Me too.' 'Me too.' 'Me too.')

They discussed a parolee who had breached his parole orders and whose parole they must revoke. Apparently the bloke had stolen a credit card, using it to buy gold jewellery and sports clothes:

'Corrective Services set him up to fail,' said someone. 'They sent him out with no methadone provider, so of course he's going to use.'

'He couldn't adapt.'

'He had no hope, this guy.'

'He was on a *massive* dose of methadone in jail, and then nothing,' said someone else.

They reached the matter of a woman guilty of murder:

'The victim's legs were found in the Georges River.'

'It was a case of sustained domestic violence suffered by the wife who eventually attacked her husband, killed him and chopped him up,' someone said.

There was a tea break. The undercover detective volunteered to buy takeaway drinks for us from the café downstairs. As he listened to our orders – cappuccino, skinny latte, soy flat white, weak cappuccino, decaf flat white, double espresso, soy macchiato, long black – he didn't confirm them or write them down and I wondered how he would remember.

Someone leafed through a newspaper and read a story about two young Australian men in an Indonesian prison who were facing execution by firing squad. 'An unfortunate situation,' he said. Andrew Chan and Myuran Sukumaran had been found guilty of being co-ringleaders of a heroin smuggling operation, which had involved seven other young Australians too, the case drawing unusual scrutiny because it had been the Australian Federal Police who had tipped off its Indonesian counterpart about the whole business, leading to the arrests. When the death penalty was announced in the Denpasar court, people had cheered.

A woman asked if I'd like to look at the notes Corrective Services had made about an inmate. I wheeled my chair over and read off her computer screen:

'Mr B_____ has no family and friends to support him. He has been employed as the sweeper in Prison Block A and has received positive reports.'

Of another inmate: 'He has completed CUBIT program and is communicating better. Whilst on parole, Mr C_____ will require extensive supervision and monitoring.'

CUBIT was the custody-based intensive treatment program for sex offenders. When I'd first heard board members use the acronym, I thought they were saying 'CUPID' and I was appalled. NSW jails had various therapeutic programs including CORE (for inmates who've committed 'low intensity' sex offences), Getting SMART (moderate intensity substance-abuse program) and Deniers. To do CUBIT or CORE, you first had to accept you committed the offence.

Deniers was for people convicted of sex offences but who maintained their innocence. It was introduced so that inmates could get access to therapeutic treatments while continuing to deny their guilt. Apparently all these programs included a 'victim empathy' component, a sort of remorse-producing ingredient. Prisoners also completed psychometric tests such as Static 99, which was designed for male sex offenders. It was a risk-assessment tool. If you rated 'high' on Static 99, your parole might be refused. The previous week, I'd downloaded Static 99 from the internet and had answered the ten questions, including 'Have you ever lived with a lover for at least two years?' ('Yes' got you zero points, 'No' got you one point) and 'Have you had any previous non-sexual violence convictions?' My overall test result was zero. I fell into the 'low-risk' category. There was no category for 'no-risk'.

The jails also ran VOTP (Violent Offenders Therapeutic Programs) for people convicted of violent crimes. I asked Parole Authority members what these various programs contained (Were the courses based purely in psychology? If so, in what way?) but no one seemed to know. Scientists had recently discovered what was being termed 'the warrior gene', a gene that affected levels of the brain chemicals dopamine and serotonin, which in turn affected men's behaviour and mood (reputedly not so for women): if you are male and have the gene, and if you have had an unstable upbringing as a child, you are more prone to violent outbursts. I had asked a judge if the gene was relevant when sentencing someone. He'd responded with his own question: if presented with a person who supposedly had it, was he expected to lock up the offender for a shorter period (because a person can't control his biology and therefore his actions are not entirely his free will), or for a longer time (because he presents more of a danger to society)? In the courts, this question had not yet been resolved.

Parole meetings were bureaucratic exercises, but they were also a study in human relations. Because only five of the twenty Authority members met at any given time, each meeting manifested its own dynamic. There was the male parole officer with pudgy cheeks who flirted benignly with the ladies, the retired researcher who brought in apples from his farm in Central New South Wales, and the strung-out woman from the attorney-general's office who occasionally forgot her security pass. I sometimes sat next to Bob Inkster, a distinguished former police detective. I liked Bob. He was someone for whom the world was a ledger precisely divided into people's right and wrong actions. During parole meetings, he didn't voice his opinions as lustily as some of the others, although his comments were sharp and always to the point. In the force he'd solved major and organised crimes, and his nickname was 'Snake' because of his patience and wits, and because, whenever he arrested a suspect, he squeezed hard and wouldn't let go.

Then there was Pike. As the benevolent alpha male, he was at his best when mentoring people. He asked them about their lives and congratulated them on their achievements. They felt nurtured by him, and so did I. He also liked to teach, whether or not the Authority members wished to be taught. A couple of times I heard him ruminate on the topic of deterrence. 'What prevents people from committing offences?' he'd ask Authority members rhetorically, swivelling his chair and leaning back. 'I don't believe it's harsh punishment. What deters people from doing something is the likelihood of getting caught,' after which he'd launch into a monologue about eighteenth-century London and public hangings ('There was a saying: pickpockets profit while thieves are being hanged!'), and about 'a very brave New South Wales police minister' who in 1982 introduced random breath testing.

During these little lectures, members were silently respectful, although sometimes I detected fidgeting, in particular from an older man who liked to sit at the other end of the table opposite Pike and challenge his views.

Members carried with them their own motives for being an Authority member, causing ripples of which they were not always aware. One former cop was sickened by the cycle of domestic violence: the abuse, the apology, the escalating abuse, the histrionics of remorse that convinces the victim to stay, then the further escalation of abuse. Another Authority member was a former alcoholic whose life had been transformed by Alcoholics Anonymous. He believed in the effectiveness of AA so completely that, at every chance, he tried to attach to an inmate's parole conditions mandatory attendance at AA. This infuriated other members who pointed out to him that the potency of AA sprang from voluntary, not compulsory, participation.

Listening quietly to all this was the young, sardonic secretary who seemed ten steps ahead of everyone else. She had degrees in psychology and criminology, she had worked as a parole officer and then as a Parole Authority member, she'd just finished a law degree and she possessed a breadth of knowledge for fast, considered decision-making. Sometimes a discussion ensued about whether or not to revoke an inmate's parole, or what date should be set for the revocation. After a few minutes, the secretary would discreetly interject, providing the clean answer everyone was flailing around for. She told me that, when she was five, her father had taken her to see Michael Chamberlain on trial in court. The moment she saw Azaria Chamberlain's tiny jumpsuit on display, she knew she wanted to become a criminal lawyer.

A faint vertigo would take hold of me during the twenty-four hours following each parole meeting. I'd arrive home, overcome by a spinning sensation that disconnected my brain from my limbs. Those evenings I'd cook rudimentary meals, but even then I burnt the garlic, or I added too much or too little liquid, and dinners were ruined. The Parole Authority members were affable people, but the hyper-efficiency of the process left me queasy. I'd expected some hand-wringing and ponderous debate, but no space was given to moral and ethical questions concerning justice and judgment, or to questions of what rehabilitation might actually mean. And it was unsettling how reliant members were on the anaemic pre-release reports written by parole officers in the jails. A few notes scratched out on a page as part of a daily workload couldn't possibly paint a portrait of a human being. During meetings I kept waiting for remorse to be mentioned, but it never was. 'The reason we don't do this by computer is to add a human element. If you're given a human judge, a human panel, then it enables discretion,' one of the members told me; 'We're just an administrative body,' said another.

The tea break ended. The detective returned with our correct coffees. 'That's a trained mind,' someone said, taking her skinny latte.

A serious sex offender who was on parole had an attitude problem.

'I wouldn't be mucking around with him,' said the female parole officer. 'When he was up for parole, butter wouldn't melt in his mouth. But since then, he's had a really bad attitude. It's something we specifically raised with him prior to release. I just want him on a really tight lead.'

They decided to stand the matter over for a progress report.

They discussed the matter of a man who was in jail for arson. He had set fire to his neighbour's house because he'd thought his neighbour was a paedophile. Later he'd discovered that the man wasn't one, and he now wanted to apologise to him. The board questioned whether the inmate needed to complete the Violent Offenders Therapeutic Program.

'Corrective Services have got him enrolled in VOTP. But is arson an act of violence?' a woman asked.

'The guy has a history of violent crimes,' said someone else, who then joked, 'or maybe the armed robbery he did all those years ago was a non-violent one.'

'But he's not in jail for armed robbery. He's in jail for arson. So why does he have to do VOTP?' said the woman.

'Was the neighbour in the house at the time?' asked somebody.

They looked over the case file and concluded that, no, the neighbour wasn't at home. What to do? Should they delay the man's parole so he could complete the program?

'I accept that he's been assessed for VOTP by psychologists,' someone said finally. 'We're not experts.'

'The programs are hard to get into, and people's parole is delayed,' said someone else, shaking his head.

Next was an awkward matter of a man whose parole they wanted to revoke; however, his actual parole period had expired a few days ago which meant that, technically, he was no longer serving his sentence.

'If we don't revoke, it sends the wrong message,' said someone.

'But it's a waste of resources to send him back to jail,' said someone else.

'How much does it cost a day to keep someone in prison?'

'Couple of hundred dollars? It's close to $80,000 a year.'

'There is so much evidence to show that, in a situation such as this, harsh penalties achieve nothing,' said the dissenter.

But he was outnumbered. Eventually the Authority decided to revoke the man's parole. They were concerned that not to do so would set a precedent. The man would do two weeks in jail.

'This is an exercise in futility,' said the outnumbered board member.

The meeting concluded at 12.30 pm. Pike and the rest of the members enacted what looked like a Greek wedding ritual: they held up bunches of paper – the lists of names of parolees and inmates, with members' accompanying comments – before ripping them into pieces and throwing them into the centre of the table. As they made for the door, an assistant wandered in and collected the scraps for shredding.

16

If you do the sort of fieldwork research I do, you chat with a person in an office or a café or a lounge room, while an audio recorder captures the exchange. The small black oblong sits on the table, but you disregard it, hoping that your interviewee has momentarily forgotten how their casual spoken words are being made data.

Later, you transcribe the discussion. The task is excruciatingly slow. It takes you eight hours to transcribe a 120-minute interview, and it is unbearable to listen to your own voice (*Shh!* you want to hiss at the interviewer with her flat vowels and flattery). Taped conversations are unsettling for they render a strip of your life sharp fact. Memory, that shape-shifting process that sculpts our here and now, is briefly lost. There's no working upon your past; no altering your backstory, no choosing to recall some moments over others, nor remembering them as soft and satiny. Transcribing the audio file forces you to *be there all over again* as you listen and re-listen, diligently typing up phrases. It's so different from reviewing home videos and family photos, the enchantment of nostalgia relying on the wistful distance between then and now (*Look at us. How young we were!*). Hearing the interview, however, and tapping out each word and half-word, entails you climb back into the exchange.

If you are fortunate and have a university research grant, you can dodge the eternal replaying of your old voice by sending the files to a professional transcription service. Days later, like magic, you receive documents in your email inbox and you print them out, the moist human conversations turned to starchy black and white. Depending on how much fieldwork you've got scheduled, and how many new lectures you must write; depending on the number of university committee meetings you must attend, the volume of student essays you must mark, and how many nights you've been awake, it may take months before you finally read the conversations, peering down onto dialogue like a fly on the wall.

*

To commit to paper ugly scenes from a marriage is to condemn both parties. No printed words can do the couple justice.

The Tasmanian trip had been medicinal, a sort of penicillin eliminating the bitterness that had afflicted Brad and me. Soon after our return, however, a new, stronger strain of hostility bloomed. Our time away together had left me ravenous for more intimate connection with my husband, so instead of avoiding the issue, I began to confront him. I was fed up with worrying about whether or not I was doing the right thing, and guessing, *inventing*, his subsequent state of mind.

The next time I noticed a scowl on his face that would not dislodge itself, I pounced.

'What's going on? What's the matter?'

'Nothing.'

'It's not nothing. You look pained.'

'Don't I always look pained?'

'Brad. C'mon. Don't do that. Let's talk.'

'*Fine*. What do you want to *talk* about?'

'What's happening with us.'

'What do you mean?'

'You *know* what I mean.'

'No I don't.'

'You do. You're angry all the time. What's going on? Let's sit down and talk about it like adults. We can't go on like this. I want us to be loving. I can't cope when you withdraw your love. I need you to be loving.'

'*I, I, I.* That's all I ever hear from you. What *you* want. What *you* need.'

'Okay, so tell me what's going on for you.'

'I'm coming down with flu, I've got to chase jobs, and it's *this* shit,' he said, flicking his hand in the direction of the kitchen.

His words were aimed at domestic duties – that morning I'd suggested he pack the dishwasher and do some food shopping – but their venom was directed at me.

He went and climbed into bed.

You've gotten what you asked for, I told myself. *You should've known it would be like this.*

Years earlier, on a Thursday night in April, when we were still living in the apartment, we'd gone to dinner at our local Italian restaurant by the beach. I'd dressed up, had worn high heels and a densely patterned turquoise and coral necklace that made me feel like Cleopatra. After our meal, we wandered up to the headland. At the white wooden fence on the sandstone rock that jutted out to the sea, Brad drew me to him. A timidity came over us. 'Will you marry me?' he asked, and I said, 'Yes.' We clutched one another. And then he said, 'Are you sure? It's going to be hard.' It had felt premonitory. I tried not to let it ruin the moment. Later, when recounting the scene to family and friends, I laughed ('Who on earth rounds off a marriage proposal with, "It's going to be hard"!?'), but his pessimism, his suspicion of joy, alarmed me.

'You don't have to stick around,' I said, following him into the bedroom. 'If this is all too much for you, if you don't want to be a part of this family, you can leave.'

'What*ever*, Kate. Let's get a divorce,' he said, eyes closed.

'Okay, Brad, yep, let's get a divorce. You say that, but you never actually do anything about it. I love you. I don't want us to separate. Life is short. One of us will die before the other one. There is no time to be anything other than loving. We can make up now, or we can keep fighting all night. Let's make up and get some sleep.'

'Great. We've made up.'

'Brad. C'mon.'

Silence.

'Can we please make up?'

'We've *made* up,' he said, ignoring me.

'Brad.'

'Tell me what to say and I'll say it.'

'C'mon.'

'Just let me sleep. Leave me alone. I'm sick.'

'I just want us to make up.'

'No you don't.'

He was right. *I* had no reason to be remorseful. What I wanted was an apology.

I heard murmuring, and crept to Jemima's door. She was having a dream. I stroked her hair and straightened the bed covers and waited until she returned to a deep sleep.

Children never really know the reasons for, or content of, their parents' quarrels. My mother's family attributed the heat between my parents to traditional enmities between Italy and Austria, as if Mum and Dad were rehearsing centuries-old conflicts; to my siblings and me, our parents' arguments were unpredictable and unfathomable. We were used to our mother's fatigue and care, and to our father's coolness interspersed with flashes of anger towards us: this was our familiar world. But we were never prepared for the asteroid strikes.

My parents' fights shook the rooms, and my sister, brother and I would stay close, finding places to take cover. Although they were not physically violent with one another, there was shouting, doors slamming, crying, and sometimes stuff was smashed and broken. The fall-out lasted days. As the eldest, I'd go from one parent to the other, imagining myself as a loom that might reweave their marriage and our home. More than once Mum came to me puffy-eyed to say that it was over this time, that she and us kids were leaving, and that I needed to pack a bag of clothes and to help my sister and brother pack bags too. Our bags were packed but we never left. After each argument, we three would wake up one morning a few days later to find our mother and father joking together in the kitchen, him pulling her to him and kissing her playfully on the forehead. Our world was restored. We were confused: *how* had love returned? The reconciliation had taken place late at night while we were asleep. My parents never sat us down and explained to us what had occurred and why. We never witnessed them making peace, saying sorry. For my mother and father, the jokes in the kitchen over breakfast erased the cataclysmic event. It was as if it had never happened.

Let Brad go to sleep, a small part of my brain was telling me as I stood outside our bedroom door. *You will both feel more generous in the morning.*

But he was being boorish. I couldn't leave it be.

'We need to make up.'

'We've made up.'

'No we haven't.'

I kept at him, refusing to let him rest until I'd gotten the 'Sorry' I wanted. It only made him wild.

At eleven o'clock he shoved a toothbrush and a change of clothes into an overnight bag. As he drove away and into the night, I stood in the garage, overrun with regret. It was self-reproach at my harassment of him (*Why didn't I rise above it*?), but mostly at the unalterable decision I had made: *This* is the person with whom I chose to have a child?

*

I lurched my way through the uni semester, the weeks a jumble of parole meetings, university classes and days with Jemima. There was a family birthday celebration for my cousin who turned eight. At the party, over fairy bread and butterfly cakes, Mum's eldest brother asked me, 'How's work?' For forty minutes I blathered on about the man who gunned down his ex-girlfriend at a Sydney casino, and whose supposed remorse was rejected by the judge; and the parolee who left jail, and who had no hope, and whose daughter found him in the bathroom, dead. That is, I talked at my poor uncle not in any contemplative, domesticated way – not in any safe way – but as a splutter of ghoulish eruptions. These lurid blobs of information from my research were unfit for tasteful conversation. They were a sort of disease I carried around like bad breath. Later I phoned him to apologise.

As for Brad and me, we'd taken three steps backwards. After spending that one night at a hotel, he'd returned the following evening. I heard the key in the door as I was getting Jemima out of the bath. He put down his bag, and came and found me.

'Can we try and make this work? I want to make this work,' he said gently.

'Yes. I want to make it work too.'

'Sorry.'

'Sorry.'

After that, we returned to not having the conversation that had to be had.

A friend of mine once told me that the arrival of a first baby is akin to throwing a grenade into a marriage. I was coming to realise that, after Jemima's birth, a history my husband and I could not see nor understand had crashed into us, our respective upbringings and origins an amassment of wayward forces. In the months after Jemima was born, I had wandered unanchored through our apartment, as if always balancing on a precipice. The psychologists who'd seen me had talked of postnatal depression, how it takes different forms, how it affects fathers too. They couldn't pinpoint the cause of the panic I felt with the baby, and it was only now, years later, I was beginning to comprehend what it might have been.

As for Brad, an inexplicable urge to escape had forever been an organising principle for him, the way an animal knows exactly when to run. When he was twelve years old he went AWOL from his parents' home to visit a girl, catching the overnight train ten hours north to Nambucca Heads, his disappearance requiring a coordinated effort by his parents, train officials, the police and the girl's family to get him back; when he was sixteen he dislodged floorboards in the built-in wardrobe in his bedroom and dug a tunnel out of the house.

Brad's grandfather was an Australian sergeant during World War II and had fought in South-East Asia. He was captured by the Japanese and spent more than three years as a prisoner-of-war in a camp at Changi before being released. Brad possesses the diary that his grandpa kept during those forty-two months, a document detailing hunger and absence, imaginary menus (*steak and kidney pies, chocolate cakes, meringues, apple sponges, custard*), and impressions of the waves rolling in at Sydney's Freshwater Beach. When Brad was nineteen, his father, age forty-nine, was diagnosed with Parkinson's disease, which had grown progressively worse throughout Brad's adulthood. His dad was someone who'd grown up with no money and who'd studied in the laundry at a tiny desk, who'd been accepted into a state selective high school, who was the first in his family to go to university, eventually becoming an architect. In other words, a person for whom mobility was synonymous with survival. Now Brad's father found it difficult to move with agency at all.

It is not possible to know every antecedent cause or contingent factor that bears upon our actions. This particular inheritance of Brad's could not completely account for my husband's behaviour – there were additional questions too about the modern roles of men and women – but it could, nonetheless, perhaps go some way to explaining it. In that first year with Jemima, I was suffering too much to consciously make these connections about Brad's life. I must have made them in a remote part of my being, because I could never shake the sense that, fundamentally, I understood him.

What held us together now was our daughter, the miracle of her. With each preschooler milestone and adorable moment, the brittleness between us deliquesced, our love for Jemima clearing a path for passion. Mostly, though, Brad spent his days melancholic, which I found both dispiriting and alluring: the heaviness and hopelessness was crushing; at the same time he was expressing the blackness in me that I could not. Men are permitted, encouraged even, to comport themselves with moroseness, a casual cynicism about the world; women less so. I felt the burden that a good wife and mother – a good female employee – feels: to be as bright as a bell.

My girlfriends knew a little of what was happening. 'Do you want another baby? Is that it?' they asked, and I said, no, that wasn't it, we only wanted one child, and, anyway, Jemima had ten cousins her age. I resisted lumping my friends with details because I was ashamed about the state of things, and afraid they would tell me to leave him, as if leaving was like ripping off a Band-Aid, and not the lifetime of heartache I suspected it would be, for I continued to love my husband ardently.

And yet what to do with the ceaseless brokenness, the longing?

When Brad and I had decided to get married, several friends had asked us why we were bothering, weddings were a fuss, and I'd responded with a short sermon on ceremony. The anthropologist in me had long recognised the power of ritual and communion, the possibility of reshaping a world when human beings share place and time. Most surprising to my friends and family was when I told them of their critical role – yes, the couple's vows were important, but their vows were important too – because even at that stage I knew it takes more than two people to make a partnership work. During our wedding, the Uniting Church minister – the family friend who years later would baptise Jemima – addressed the congregation, asking everyone whether they supported this marriage, to which our loved ones responded: 'We do.'

Now, years on, I tried returning to how I'd felt during that forty-minute ceremony: the sense of us being held by something much greater than ourselves.

The people with whom I most shared my sentiments were my sister and brother, who lived far away and whom I missed terribly, and my mum, who like me was a writer, which meant we could talk about books we'd read, and pieces we were working on, and how much of a slog it was putting one word after another. I was used to phoning her around five o'clock when the hours of light slipped away; ever since Brad's night at the hotel, however, my phone calls to her had become twice or more a day. I felt bad for how much I leant on her; and, in tender moments with Brad, I felt guilty, for it was as if I was having an illicit affair with my mother behind my husband's back.

Mum took those phone calls without judgment of either him or me. She just listened. Then she said that life was long, that relationships required stamina; that I was part of the larger feminist project, and I should be firm about the things I could change, and accepting of those I could not; and that, since I still loved Brad, it was important I remained loving. A close girlfriend, who had older kids, said the same thing: that these early years with a small child were so tough on a couple, and that no parent should ever make a major life decision (buying a house, getting a divorce) when their child is under five years of age, because the parent is not mentally stable.

I had stamina. I did. What I couldn't stomach, though, was what seemed a dismaying reality of marriage: that you could have love, or you could have justice, but not both.

As Brad and I lumbered along, I calculated the months until Jemima's fifth birthday – eleven or thereabouts – and I wondered if things would get better.

17

Over the following months I observed more than a hundred parole hearings. I patiently waited for remorse to make a commanding appearance, but it remained elusive, existing as hearsay or not at all.

The layout in Courtroom 4.07 of the Sydney West Trial Courts building, where hearings were held, was reminiscent of a modern art installation. More than twenty screens sat on tables, with several attached to the walls, and on them was the live image of a man wearing a green tracksuit. He sat at a little desk. Behind him was a handwritten sign ('Silverwater') showing which jail the courtroom technology had beamed into. He fidgeted, and the synchronised screens leapt to life.

A giant window to my right let in barrels of sunlight. An assistant from the Parole Authority whom I'd not met before approached me.

'Are you here for a particular matter?' he asked.

'No, I'm a researcher,' I told him.

He was pleased as punch. He handed me an information booklet about the parole process. Did I know that New South Wales was the only jurisdiction in the Asia-Pacific region to have public hearings? It's all about transparency! Had I seen this technology? Inmates used to appear in person, but now they appeared via an audiovisual link from one of twenty-seven videoconferencing studios in twenty-two correctional centres across the state. It was a *cost-effective* means of having offenders in court.

Ian Pike and four other Authority members entered the courtroom. We all stood, including the inmate on the screens, the camera's framing having the unfortunate effect of beheading him.

The Parole Authority listened to the inmate's lawyer before leaving the room to deliberate whether or not to release him.

A savvy young Legal Aid lawyer explained to me how, when representing inmates at parole hearings, he built a remorse sketch. With his finger, he pointed in the air to dots on an imaginary timeline: 'I locate the point in time when the offence was committed, then the point in time when the offender felt sorry for the offence, and the point in time when I can say, "Now, looking back . . .". These are the points you want to find in order to construct a narrative around.'

In court I listened for this rhetorical arc. Sometimes I gleaned it ('Saints in the Christian Church were scumbags before they were saints!' I heard one lawyer declare. 'My client's life is *totally* changed!') But mostly I was aware of the astonishing absence of what was surely supremely important: the offender's voice.

I grew used to seeing on the screens the expressionless faces of men, their hands clasped in front of them like good boys. Often the audiovisual link dropped out, and there were phone calls between staff in the jails and in the courtroom as they tried to fix it; or the camera clumsily zoomed in and out, giving the framing the flavour of a Lars von Trier film. These hearings were supposed to see the Parole Authority and the inmate enacting a meaningful, human exchange, and yet lawyers told me that in jail the inmates looked at a split screen (images of the judge's bench, counsel and part of the public seating) uncertain where they were meant to focus their gaze; that the audio played up, which meant the men lost half of what was being said in court; and that inmates also contended with the background noise in the jails: metal doors clanging, the shouting and fighting.

The prisoners had no control over how they were – literally – being presented. Concerned about the limitations of the technology, a lawyer said to me: 'It's much harder to lock someone up if they are standing right in front of you. But the AV link is better than nothing.'

During one hearing, a psychologist's report was submitted to the Parole Authority. The court learnt that the inmate had 'anti-social attitudes', 'a propensity to engage in risk-taking behaviour', and that he was only halfway through the Violent Offenders Therapeutic Program. The guy was doing time for malicious intent to cause grievous bodily harm. His lawyer argued in a long-winded way that 'all was not how it appeared' and that the fellow wasn't so bad. When the Authority members left to deliberate, the lawyer muttered, 'Fucking psychologist's report.' I couldn't help but notice one other thing that should have concerned him: early into the hearing, the video link had faltered, which meant that throughout those twenty minutes, a frozen image of the cross-armed inmate wearing an accidental menacing grimace had dominated the screens around the room. The Authority returned and announced that the guy's parole was refused.

The hearings varied time-wise, although they were usually dispensed with haste. Pike sounded benevolent, in a brisk way, and tried to let people down gently if they didn't get paroled, which was the case in most of the matters.

Inmates were, technically, given the chance to say something to the court, but few did. When they did speak, their performances were disastrous.

One guy had recently had his parole revoked for breaching the conditions of his release, namely missing meetings with his parole officer and failing to attend a therapeutic program. At his parole hearing, his counsel argued for his re-release, explaining that the inmate had arrived to meet his parole officer and waited for several hours, but the officer never appeared. The court also learnt that the man didn't attend the Managing Emotions Therapeutic Program because, on one day, his car broke down, and on another, he had to attend a funeral.

At the end of the evidence, Ian Pike asked the man if there was anything he'd like to add. The room fell silent. Everyone looked at the man on the screen.

'Um . . .' the inmate said, with the look of panic people get when they know something is expected of them, but they're not sure what. 'I'm really sorry for what I done?' he offered, pathetically.

The Authority retired for a few minutes before returning to court and announcing that the man's application for re-release was rejected.

The man was young, inarticulate and Aboriginal.

When I'd interviewed judges, some had spoken about the disadvantages faced by Indigenous Australians caught up in the system, the ongoing effects of our nation's history: land dispossession and the displacement of people, the forced removal of children from their families, intergenerational poverty and trauma. The judges had reiterated how Aboriginal people were grossly overrepresented in our nation's jails. They spoke, too, of cultural difference. I was told that a sort of 'cheat sheet' had been sent around to the judges, informing them to be sensitive to the ways in which Indigenous Australians presented themselves in court.

'Aborigines, we are told, and it is certainly borne out in my experience, sometimes have difficulty, culturally, looking people in the eye,' one elderly judge had said. 'And they can look shifty in court. It would be very wrong to discount their evidence because they didn't measure up to the standard test for whether someone's telling the truth: that is, whether they look you in the eye.'

'It took decades for judges to be educated that the demeanour of an Indigenous person might not reflect guilt,' said another.

These comments, and others, had sounded well-intentioned, and jejune.

The criminal courts claimed to want to see people's true selves, but what they really wanted were smooth comportments, undisturbed sincerity. People, like David whom I'd interviewed, were familiar with the genre: when he had stood in court and when the judge had asked him about his crime, he'd sensed the precise enactment required of him. Other people, though, found themselves at the centre of an exotic ritual, clueless of the rules.

At one hearing, an elderly Malay man with little English appeared on the screens. His interpreter, a Malay woman, sat in the witness box and solemnly swore to translate English to Cantonese and Cantonese to English. The inmate suddenly spoke, which set off a fugue-like exchange, three voices and two languages overlapping.

'I want to say something,' said the interpreter translating the inmate's words.

We heard Cantonese from him.

'The officer will read a letter to Your Honour,' said the interpreter.

The man had written a letter. He wanted the prison officer who was standing near him in the jail to read it to the court.

His lawyer interrupted, confused: 'This is a new development.'

More Cantonese from the man.

'Just a few sentences,' said the interpreter.

Cantonese.

'To ask for leniency,' she said.

'I had an audiovisual conference with my client yesterday,' interjected the inmate's lawyer. The lawyer had thought that his client understood what would happen today.

Cantonese.

'Only a few sentences. I ask the court for leniency,' the interpreter said.

'I explained to my client that —'

He was cut off by more Cantonese.

'I'm not going to make any complaint or defend myself. I'm just going to ask for leniency,' said the interpreter.

Ian Pike assumed control, the voices ceased, and we didn't hear from the inmate again.

In rare moments, I would witness a prisoner unadorned: a single self unencumbered by display. One morning, an inmate's wife and three little boys, his mother, his brothers and sisters-in-law, occupied the first two rows of the public seating. Their husband, brother, father appeared on the screens, and they gave him a little wave. The man's lawyer argued his client's case, and the Parole Authority left the courtroom to deliberate over lunch.

Now the inmate was alone with his family. His face relaxed, discarding its shell of solemnity. His two youngest sons, four and six years old, crept over to the microphone and began speaking to their father.

'Hi Dad,' the youngest said, grinning into the camera.

'Can't wait to see you, bubba,' the man gushed. 'You're getting big!'

'I love you,' said the other boy.

'I love you, I miss you,' said their dad.

The tiny conversation was on loudspeaker and the inmate's devoted expression filled the screens on the walls and desks. The third boy, the eldest, didn't follow his brothers to the camera. He clung to his mother's leg and wept.

During lunch I joined the Parole Authority members. Shaken, I told them what I'd seen and I suggested they release this man. One member, a police detective, regarded my wet face.

'Kate, you can't catch crooks with sooks,' he told me.

'He's an armed robber!' the others said. 'He's had sixty-one prior convictions!'

I felt gormless for saying anything, naïve for believing in the power of familial love to effect personal change, and I limply attended to my sandwich.

Back in the courtroom forty minutes later, the family returned to their seats. The spent children leant their floppy heads and bodies on whichever relative was closest. Pike announced that the inmate would be released in two weeks, after which the man would complete a rehabilitation program. I gave a silent little cheer.

'You have had a long and unhappy history,' he told the inmate. 'You have to turn yourself around 180 degrees.' Pike thanked the man's family for coming along today: 'A strong family base helps to keep people on the straight and narrow.'

Outside court, the man's brother high-fived the other relieved adults, and together they spoke of plans and celebration. Their guy was getting out!

The three small boys, however, looked blank-faced.

'Daddy will be home in *two weeks*!' their uncle told them.

But fourteen days was a lifetime to a child. The boys glanced searchingly through the courtroom door, and around the large empty foyer. They had expected to have their father back today, their dad magically climbing out of the television, scrambling over the tables and chairs, and rushing to hold them.

18

Insomnia renders a person all body. I was teeth and gums. The ache in the mouth was the self's inability to bite off and chew bits of experience, to make sense of them.

Were I living elsewhere, among people who looked to other heavens, perhaps my sleeplessness might have been diagnosed: 'soul loss'. A shaman would have divined its origin and seen how, without my knowing, a sudden fright had caused my spirit to flee, the thing escaping from my mouth, disappearing and wandering loose in the world. Then he would have tracked down my lost soul and called it back into my body.

At the university I camouflaged this absence by producing research papers. I quarantined sections of fieldwork data, slicing them up for analysis, and when my articles began appearing in academic journals, my managers said, 'Keep up the good work.'

In bed thoughts flung themselves at me.

Can remorse be wrenched from time? Is it only ever retrospective? Can it be forward-looking? Can it flood you in advance of what might occur, and of your utter failure to stop it?

At three o'clock one morning, I opened the front door and crept out into the cold air. I stood on the deck for a few moments, my eyes adjusting to the gloom. Something was dangling from the magnolia tree. I could see a long cord at the end of which was a small object. Had a kid hurled a ball on a strap into our yard? I looked closer. The object was kidney-shaped, the rope to which it was attached was twisted and slimy. Oh God, animal entrails. Probably a possum's. Revolted and intrigued, and confused as to what predator was responsible, I moved towards it, watching it spin slowly. I was instantly nauseous. No, not a kidney. A foetus. A possum-birth gone wrong. The baby creature hung suspended from its umbilical cord, newly dead.

I went back to bed. In the morning I'd dispose of the corpse.

*

During a parole meeting there began a discussion among Authority members that I wished I could audio-record. They had gotten through the As and the Bs, and they were onto the Cs, when they reached the case of Samuel Connor.

Six and a half years ago, on the day of his twenty-first birthday, Connor was drunk and high. He sped down a road on the outskirts of his hometown in inland New South Wales, and struck a pole. He woke up in hospital with fractured ribs, a punctured lung and a broken hip, to learn that he'd killed three friends and seriously injured a fourth. He pleaded guilty to three counts of manslaughter, and one count of dangerous driving causing grievous bodily harm, and was sentenced to eight years in jail, with a non-parole period of four years. He was granted parole a few months ago.

'I want to give him a slap,' said a female parole officer.

Connor had breached the conditions of his parole order. He'd not been allowed to consume alcohol, but he kept being caught drinking at his local pub. He'd already been given a warning.

'He's saying we have ruined his social life. I want to give him more than a warning; I want to call him up,' the woman said.

'Yes, there are concerns there,' said someone else.

'Just his *attitude*,' she continued. 'And it's in the area where the victims' families live. Can you imagine if your son was killed and you saw this guy at the pub?'

'In the pre-release report it states that he's devastated he had to kill his friends in order to learn a lesson. But he *hasn't learnt*. He's *not sorry*,' said another member.

'In those country towns there isn't a lot to do. He doesn't have the ability to expand his horizons beyond the pub,' said someone else.

They decided to give him a face-to-face warning – a 'sound warning', said the young woman – and set a date for a parole hearing, where Connor would present evidence as to why he should be allowed to continue to serve the remainder of his sentence in the community and not in prison.

It was what I'd been waiting for: the promise of an actual offender in-the-flesh, standing in front of the Parole Authority; the physical conditions that might give rise to remorse and restoration. I scribbled the date in my diary.

A judge I'd spoken with had referred to calamities like Samuel Connor's as 'There-but-for-the-grace-of-God accidents'. Any one of those young people could have been driving. But after the crash, as Connor was led away to prison, the families of the perished kids had criticised what they saw as his lenient sentence. 'We have to live without our children,' one mother had said. 'My son is not coming back. He's never ever going to come back.'

After the meeting, I drove to the university. I had a pile of marking to get through. Sitting at my desk with student essays, my attention kept veering to Connor's case and the agony of those parents. There was nowhere for their pain to go.

A colleague popped into my office to say hello. I told him about the Parole Authority, and we talked about the justice system and about punishment.

'Prison is the hell at the centre of your research,' he told me.

I nodded. But as he walked away, I knew he was wrong. He was a father. He had kids. He'd not thought it through.

*

Brad and I stopped sleeping in the same bed. The sound of his night-time breathing had always been for me an animal comfort. Now the snoring shook my brain.

I lay in the spare room on a mattress on the floor. The nocturnal solitude was miserable. I strong-armed my imagination towards visions of calm, but it kept sprouting recollections of Jemima's infancy. My memory of her newborn months was overlaid with shame, for a chasm lay between the mother I had expected to be, and the mother I was. I'd expected to love her; to feel a more intense version of the feeling I'd always associated with the term 'love': I loved my parents, siblings, nieces, nephews; I loved my husband. I had expected my sentiments for the baby would be in the same category of thing, just more vivid. Instead, what I felt when she was born frightened me. 'Love' was too tame a word for it. What I felt was wild, uncivilised, insane.

We are at the hospital. It's a Friday, early morning. The baby is coming.

My hips stretch and stretch and I separate, and our fresh child is placed on my chest. I raise a tiny leg to peep, 'It's a girl! We have a girl!' and we weep, and our crumple-faced daughter who is not quite yet 'Jemima', for we haven't entirely settled on a name, grips my finger and peers up at me. Time and my body become strange. Minutes and seconds do not pass. I am larger than the room, more immense than the oceans and skies beyond the window. This must be how God feels.

Late that day at the hospital a malign inversion occurred, for calm turned to dread: the baby was outside my skin. Jemima lay in her official transparent plastic cot, but I needed her close. So on Saturday before dawn, when I'd not slept for forty-eight hours, I lifted her to me and signed a form releasing the hospital of responsibility should she fall out of my bed or be crushed by my flaccid weight. The form assumed I might drift into unconsciousness, leaving my child to her own oblivion.

For the next three days, and for many months afterwards, I barely slept. I wasn't worried that the baby *might* die. I was convinced she *would*. I drifted to and from her cot, checking for breath. Mum told me to imagine God cradling our girl so that I might relax and slumber. But to picture it tempted fate, wishing my baby to heaven. Instead, in the night I sat on our red sofa and held her, stroking her tiny, velvety face. Sometimes I succumbed to rest and slept fitfully. Jemima cheeped and I was on my feet before I'd registered the sound. It wasn't me – the cognisant me – who heard her. It was my hard breasts. They wrenched me out from under the winter blankets and jerked me upright. My head wasn't its usual thing: a container for and generator of thoughts. My skull felt mangled as if from a bomb blast, one eye receding into its socket, the other eye floating ten centimetres from my face. I no longer experienced myself as a mind reflecting on the world but as pulsing Pavlovian body bits.

The demented exhaustion meant that superstition seized me. Each day at dusk I invested Jemima's stuffed toys with the force of angels and prayed they'd guard her, calling on my grandmother's ghost to do the same. After sundown, realising my impotence to absorb whatever potential malignancies might visit my child, I whimpered, defeated. Then I ran bath after bath, taking two or three a night, as if the hot water might make me whole.

We were living in our apartment at the headland. During bleak hours, I thought the cliffs were crying out to me. They'd cried out to others: those poor people who were pulled to them by something almighty and whose wretched corpses were found in the sea by the searchlights of rescue helicopters.

One night my despair led Brad to call in a doctor who stood in our kitchen at midnight and gave me a sleeping tablet, which I didn't take, for it would have affected my milk. The man tried to grasp my hopelessness but I had no means to articulate the plainest fact: that this baby, whom I'd kept safe under folds of fat and sinew, was now undefended.

19

We bundled bags and our four-year-old girl into the car, left the coast and headed west. It was a five-hour drive to the town of Wagga Wagga; with rest breaks, it would take six.

I'd considered travelling alone, Brad and Jemima remaining at home for two nights without me. But I didn't want to be apart from them. Not for this trip.

On the motorway we were soon passing gold bursts of wattle, smoky gums and hard blue sky; we were bound for the grasslands, the flood-and-drought country that surrounds Australia's scorched desert centre, a limit-place for living creatures.

Jemima shut her eyes and settled into sleep.

A week earlier, I'd spent a morning with a woman called Martha Jabour. She was a member of the Parole Authority, a victims' rights representative. I'd sat next to her during meetings, noticing her black, billowing outfits and burgundy lipstick, and how the others deferred to her when discussing violent cases. She'd told me about an upcoming parole hearing, which I'd subsequently attended. A young man had spent ten years in prison for aggravated sexual assault and manslaughter: he'd suffocated a young woman at a party. The girl's parents – shrivelled, misshapen – had attended the court session;

there too was the inmate's mother, heavy and grey. We all heard about the prisoner's model performance in jail, and of his remorse, and that he was to be granted parole. The matter concluded, the girl's mother and father rose from their seats, borne out and away. I'd stayed there alone in court, sunlight beating on the glass.

To sit in a room with the families of the killer and the killed demands a depth of courage I'm not certain I possess. The walls of the courtroom, so ordinary, so *orderly*, must somehow carry within them cosmic rupture. What to do with the breach? An Australian judge once wrote of the duty of forgiveness. In the justice system, he argued, the act of forgiveness was unrelated to the duty of punishment; it was not the role of the courts to forgive a person, 'forgiveness is not a judge's business'; only the victims can forgive. Could a person's remorse ever be something out of which could be constructed lumpy stitches of reconciliation? Surely contrition was useless when stripped of its capacity to repair.

Martha had always exuded a great deal of warmth, but until recently I'd avoided speaking with her in any intimate way for fear of appearing disrespectful, and of what I might be told. It was the fear of contracting another person's sorrow.

She and I sat down together to talk one morning in an office space in Parramatta. Martha was doing the work she did with victims and their families because, twenty-five years ago, her baby son had died of sudden infant death syndrome. He was seven weeks old when she checked on him in his cot one day and he was lifeless.

To cope with the grief, to tame and understand it, to try to ameliorate it in others, Martha underwent training and became a volunteer counsellor for the SIDS Association. At each call-out, she would sit with the traumatised parents in their home, helping them hand over their dead baby to ambulance officers. One day a mother lamented to Martha that she and her husband had taken hundreds of photos of their first child, but not many of their second, the one who'd just died and whose body had been taken away. Martha offered to help. At the mortuary she photographed the baby. She took handprints and footprints in ink, and she took a lock of hair. This retrieval practice became her job: with the mortuary attendants, she would dress the baby and take photos. She would bring the baby back to life for an hour.

For years Martha thought that SIDS was every parent's nightmare. Then she met families of murdered children, including the mother and father of a nine-year-old girl who, while walking home from school, had been abducted, raped and killed. The families had felt peripheral to legal processes, an afterthought of the courts. They'd battled to understand what was happening and why, so they founded an association – the Homicide Victims' Support Group – that they asked Martha to coordinate. It was the first of its kind in Australia, if not the world, and was formed to campaign for victims' rights and to guide families through the justice system.

Martha was now the director of the association. During our conversation, she handed me a bunch of monthly newsletters. I read tributes to lost husbands, wives, mothers, fathers, brothers, sisters, sons, daughters, and was thumped by the pain: 'There is a terrible, empty void. Time does not heal', 'Another birthday without you', 'You were taken too early', 'I have ridden out a murderous summer of grief'.

Martha directed me to a front-page story written by a woman called Debbie Irons whose brother was murdered twenty years ago. Placed next to the text was a photo of a gentle-looking kid, barely out of his teens, dressed in a navy-blue suit with a gardenia pinned to his lapel.

'Our next support group meeting is in Wagga Wagga,' Martha said. 'If you want to hear how a person learns to live with murder, what they do with a perpetrator's remorse, you should speak with Debbie. She will be there. You should come.'

*

They say that our curiosity about other people's tragedy satisfies a desire in us we barely understand. My friend, a memoirist, reflected on Anne Carson's work, and wrote that perhaps our voyeurism 'enables us to imagine our own reactions in a dark well of horror. It lets us watch others suffer. By watching, we are prepared. By watching, we place a frame around our world and pace its boundaries.' This is true, I think, the boundary-pacing; it's the pacing we do when witnessing our peers being punished. But the voyeurism can be about other things too, things unseen by you until they are ready to give themselves up.

The birth of my baby had altered space and time in ways I was still trying to comprehend. She had been inside me; now there she was in her hospital cot, isolated. This realisation was the sudden fright that caused my spirit to flee. From that moment, the spectre of Jemima's death tormented me. Something such as SIDS could strike without reason or warning. It epitomised the utter randomness of life's events.

Throughout my pregnancy, nothing had felt random. The instant the magic blue line appeared on the white stick, I tumbled into a relentless happiness I had never known before, nor since. It was the result of hormones, of eating well and with abandon, and of an unarticulated logic: the foetus was perfectly safe, for my womb was its own simple universe with its own physical rules; a world of cellular division and symmetry, of order. I'd subscribed to an online pregnancy newsletter, receiving weekly announcements in my inbox: *your baby's heart and blood vessels are fully formed; your baby's eyes can blink*. Whenever I used the verb 'developing' – 'The baby is developing' – I never pictured possibles, only certainties, the elegant unfolding of a maths solution.

When the baby spilled out of me, she left the calm world of numbers and entered *our* world, a universe with unpredictable phenomena. Things could *happen* to her. As I stared at the creature in the hospital cot, a new logic asserted itself: if I remained alert, I could keep my baby safe; if I remained awake, I could arrest chaos itself.

Jemima was five months old when she and I spent four nights at a family care centre. The place had a waitlist but I was shoehorned into it after a routine baby check-up. A nurse had noticed I couldn't stop crying, and had me complete a questionnaire that assessed mothers' mental health.

The centre was on the other side of town in a run-down federation building with dozens of rooms like a ramshackle manor. Brad drove us there, and when he was due to leave, he gripped my hand, which had been adorned with a thin plastic hospital wristband, and told me everything would be alright.

The other women seemed nice, but I was in no state to make friends. There was Hira, a Turkish immigrant, with her petite, wide-eyed seven-month-old daughter, Azra, who she called 'My forty-minute girl' because, day and night, the baby only ever slept in forty-minute blocks; Diane with Liberty, an eleven-week-old infant with a turned-up nose, a shock of brown hair like a bad toupee, and angry blue eyes; Georgie from California, who spoke loudly and warmly and who cried about her daughter who'd been born seven weeks premature; and there was South African Lucy, tall with alabaster skin, who looked like someone from another time, and who listed to us the correct parenting techniques she'd used with her son and was therefore at a loss to fathom his refusal to cooperate. As they all congregated in the dining area and chatted, I sat on my bed holding Jemima and tried to breathe. At night, she and I were separated. She slept in a cot in her own room along a corridor of babies; I was in another section with the mothers. If she woke for a feed, a nurse would fetch me. Her wellbeing was in the hands of strangers. For the first two nights I lay awake straining to hear her, and counted the minutes between each clang of the bathroom door outside my room. But then, as I got to know the nurses, I imagined them as fairy godmothers watching over my child.

I saw the resident psychologist, a winsome woman in her forties with silky hair and dimples. Her office was at the highest point of the building, at the top of several flights of stairs, like Rapunzel's tower, and it had a window to the sky. I was there to account for my panic and despair, so I talked. I told her about my father, of my childhood home, and how I had never felt safe. I told her stories of 1940s Europe and of occupied cities, stories that weren't stories but real horrors seen and felt by children who, thirty years later in a country on the other side of the world, would involuntarily pass on the legacy to their children. I told her I'd grown up feeling I should be forever ready to pack my bag and go; how, now, I could grab the baby, press her close and run.

After my stay at the centre I had temporarily found a way to sleep. Jemima began on solid food, she filled out, developing a robustness typical of chubby, upright-sitting babies. She was strong, and stationary. I fantasised she would remain that way. But life is not static; it is defined by irreversible process. And it is messy. Life relies on change, the pull towards entropy, disorder.

A year after being at that centre, this new insomnia had arrived, the one that had driven me to the criminal courts. It was when Jemima had begun walking. She and I had been in the lounge room in our apartment one afternoon when I'd whispered, 'What about if you walk into the study and say hello to Daddy?' She flashed me a gummy grin, steered her little body around in a five-point turn, and started tottering unaided. 'She's on her way to see you!' I called to Brad. From that point we no longer had a baby in our home but an actual person with motion and stride. She was a human agent with her own momentum.

Her movement delighted me, and it was terrifying. Until then I had conceived of chaos as if it was external to my infant. Chaos was 'out there'. It could visit her. Suddenly, with no warning, *she* had become a random, unstoppable force.

My mother says that Jemima takes after me, that I was this sort of child, and that my father was too: fast-moving, deeply physical. Once children are walking, you cannot control the ways in which they launch themselves into the world, nor how the world bodies forth and enmeshes them. I was three when I became lost in Wytham Woods. We were living in Oxford and had set out walking to explore bluebells and twisted oak trees, when off I ran. My parents called out. No response. I wasn't running away from, or towards, anything. It was an infant's impulse, the pounding of legs and heart. My parents kept calling out, but the forest air couldn't carry their cries quite far enough, and during those long minutes until I returned unharmed, no echo sounded. Their child's voice was gone.

20

It was dusk when we pulled into the driveway of the serviced apartments in Wagga Wagga. Children on scooters careened through the narrow car park as we unpacked our luggage and went upstairs to our room.

The next morning, Brad took Jemima to the playground while I set out on foot, the Murrumbidgee River guiding my route. The path was muddy, bands of mosquitos hovering along the water's edge. Five months ago in these parts, it had begun to rain and had not stopped, the heaviest deluge on record. Wagga residents had monitored the bulging river, its body rising so fast and with such force, until finally they were told to flee and 9000 people were evacuated. The levee near the city area held strong, but not so downstream, for the river broke its banks, and locals could do nothing but gape as the muddy liquid rushed through the suburbs, blanketing roads and homes. Then the long wait began. The water had to go somewhere, somehow, and it did, eventually receding, and one day the town was almost dry and the river had returned to its familiar size.

I reached the RSL club, a slick-looking complex, and was shown into a boardroom where the Homicide Victims' Support Group was scheduled to meet. Ten high-backed leather seats were stationed around a long table, and a wooden clock hung on the wall with the Union Jack and Australian flags framing it.

Martha arrived, followed by four women and a man. The women, in their forties and fifties, kissed and hugged, inquiring after one another's families, sharing news, while the man, who was a bit older, hung about awkwardly before taking a seat next to me.

Martha began the meeting by acknowledging any birthdays or anniversaries of the people who'd been killed. I expected the assembly to follow a usual agenda, and that I would unobtrusively observe goings-on, but Martha immediately introduced me as a researcher from Sydney, after which everyone adopted the attention of obedient students. Put on the spot, I spoke in a disorganised way about my work, how I was interested in remorse. I hoped this would prompt loose, thoughtful reflection. Instead, my presence set in train a series of practised narratives.

One woman told me the story of her 71-year-old mother who was killed by three men. Her sister's partner had arranged it, he was one of them, she said. The men broke into her mother's house, stuffed undies in her mouth, taping it, before placing a pillowcase over her head, binding her hands and feet, and tying her to a chair. They grabbed all the cash they could find, and left. It took ten days for her mum to die. The men were so stupid: they'd stolen the old paper money no longer in circulation. They went on a spending spree and were traced to Queensland where they were arrested. The youngest guy immediately confessed. The other two tried to pin the whole thing on their young mate. They were convicted of murder, but appealed it and the conviction was reduced to manslaughter. They'd never intended for her mother to die. After the robbery they'd made a 000 phone call so that police would rescue her, but the emergency services had treated the call as a prank and hadn't logged it.

'None of the men have ever said "Sorry",' the woman said. 'Even if they were sobbing on the floor, I wouldn't believe them.'

The others nodded.

'Criminals shouldn't get a discount for remorse,' she continued. 'It's just morally right to show remorse. If I was distracted while driving and accidentally killed someone's child, then it wouldn't matter to the child's family if I was sorry or not. The child is dead. The family will hate me forever, no matter what I do. If the men who killed Mum were remorseful, they wouldn't have done it in the first place.'

'Everyone's sorry,' said another woman stonily. She told me the story of her sister who, twenty years ago, was beaten to death by her boyfriend. Since then, she and her husband had raised her sister's children. She wasn't happy with the judge's sentence, which she saw as too lenient.

'I want to know if judges actually consult with one another. Where is the consistency?' she asked, before catching herself. 'At least we got a conviction,' she said quietly.

The woman was keenly aware of the man in the room. He spoke up: 'Martha, is my son's case closed? Or does it remain an unsolved homicide case?' Then he turned to me: 'The guy who killed my son admitted, "I got the knife and used it on him." He's never said he was sorry.'

This father tried to tell me about what had happened to his 35-year-old son, but was unable to order events chronologically. The event was so recent – barely two years ago – that he had no narrative purchase. As he stumbled through disjointed details, I tried stringing together a meaningful sequence: his son was walking home from a mate's place when a stranger stabbed him in the heart; the perpetrator confessed, arguing it was self-defence, but the man's son wasn't carrying a weapon, only a wallet and handkerchief; in court the defendant didn't show any remorse, he just waved and smiled at everyone, and the father wanted to throw up on him; the defendant's testimony was inconsistent, but for some reason that no one can understand, the jury found him not guilty; the father reckoned that, after seven days of deliberating, the jury were tired and they just wanted to go home.

This father was worried that the man might kill someone else. He worried that another family might go through what his family was going through. He and his daughter wanted the case reopened. They had written letters to anyone they thought might help: the government, the opposition. But the other day his daughter had told him she had to try to move on with her life, that it was destroying her to invest everything in trying to fix this, and that she could see it was destroying him too.

'But I have to keep pursuing the case,' the father told us. 'I need to honour my son. I won't be honouring him if I give up.'

The room lapsed into silence.

'Isn't grief a terrible thing,' said one woman softly. 'It eats away at you.'

'Yes,' the father whispered.

No one said anything.

Eventually the father spoke: 'One night after his death, I heard footsteps on the verandah. I went outside and saw a shadow retiring into the fog. I sensed it was my son.'

'I know my brother is around,' said another woman who hadn't spoken much and who I later learnt was Debbie Irons. 'I talk to him all the time.'

'Are we psycho?' asked the father.

'No!' they all answered.

Martha gauged the mood, people's retreat into memory, and called the meeting to an end.

As they all left, Debbie remained behind. We sat together at the corner of the table, and I saw for the first time how slight she was and how loosely her clothes hung on her.

'I have to be careful what I say in front of some of the others,' she said. 'A lot of people won't reach the place I've reached. Some of their loved ones' murders are just horrible.' She told me that, as strange as it sounds, her family was lucky because her brother was killed instantly, the police knew who did it, they had the man in custody, the court case happened quickly and 'we got a good sentence'.

As Debbie began her story, I saw the work that time does for self-narration, how it gives form to a life. Like the other women at the meeting earlier, she had had more than a decade to grow herself around her torment and find a way to chronicle it. Through her repeated telling of events, she had refined and polished the story, and now the story could do its work independently of the teller. It meant that, unlike that poor father, she no longer had to relive the debilitating pain.

In 1991, Debbie was twenty-four and pregnant with her second child when her younger brother Michael was killed. He had been a long-time friend of a fellow called Glen. They lived in a small town north-east of Wagga. One night, the friends played darts at a local pub before going home. Some time after midnight, Glen arrived at Michael's place with a rifle and a double-barrelled shotgun. He shot the left barrel into the wall. Then he reloaded and shot Michael.

Glen drove an hour to his grandmother's house. He told her what happened, and that he was sorry because Michael was his best mate. He handed himself in to police, but pleaded not guilty to murder, saying that he'd gone to Michael's house that night to sell him the guns, and that it was an accident, manslaughter. But there was a witness who'd seen Glen shoot Michael.

At the murder trial, Glen shook and cried. As he stood there in the dock, Debbie watched him and thought: *These jury people are looking at this terrified 24-year-old who is saying, 'I killed my best mate.'* He wasn't remorseful, though. He was scared of what was going to happen to him.

Glen was found guilty and sentenced to sixteen years in prison, twelve years non-parole. But he appealed it, arguing that he was drunk and tired when police had obtained his account of the killing, and that, because of his mental and physical condition, this account was unreliable. Debbie worried his appeal would be upheld. She attacked him in court, screaming: 'You are not going to get away with this! I won't allow it!' Court officers ran towards her to hold her back. Glen's appeal was dismissed.

Debbie became angry and bitter. She couldn't grieve for Michael because whenever she thought of her brother, Glen occupied her thoughts. She had never felt hate before, but now Glen had given her fear and he'd given her hate. She fantasised about killing him once he left prison: pouring honey on him and tying him to an ants' nest; infecting him with the AIDS virus. She wanted to visit Glen in jail but she wasn't allowed to. Correctional Services had a duty of care to protect him. So she wrote to him. She sent him Michael's twenty-first birthday card. She wrote to him telling him how much she hated him and that she hoped he was suffering every day. Glen wrote back. Debbie sat on the riverbank and read and re-read his letter, convinced he'd been coached in writing it. It was full of excuses. He reiterated that he'd gone to Michael's place to sell the guns and that one had gone off. He wrote: 'It was a tragic event of Shakespearian proportions'.

Debbie's family was Catholic. When Michael died she went to a priest and said, 'I really hate this guy Glen.' As a Catholic, you are supposed to forgive and forget, which was what the priest told her: 'Mary forgave them for killing Jesus. You have to forgive Glen.' Debbie struggled with this. She needed permission to hate. Her family reacted differently. Her mother was shattered, broken. She aged overnight. Her sister fell apart too. Her father drank. He wasn't sober for five years after Michael's death. He said he lost his faith. He couldn't believe in God anymore.

Eight months after Michael was murdered, Debbie gave birth. The nurses handed her the baby, but she couldn't love him because she was terrified she might lose him. 'Please take him away,' she told them.

She became a paranoid mother who couldn't let her children out of her sight. She would have panic attacks and couldn't go grocery shopping. She would arrive at the supermarket and have to lock herself in the car. She put on a lot of weight. She broke out in cold sores, her dermatitis played up, and her eyes started twitching. She ended up with lupus.

Debbie saw that losing someone to homicide was different from other sorts of loss and grief. To start with, you're ashamed. People would ask her, 'Do you have brothers and sisters?' She'd answer that she had a sister and a brother who's deceased. They would ask, 'Was it a car accident?' She would tell them, 'He was murdered,' and people would immediately step back from her as if to say, *What sort of family do you come from?* Before Michael was killed, Debbie used to think the same way: *What did the person do to get murdered?*

Eleven years after Michael's death, Glen was eligible to apply for parole. Debbie's family made a submission to the state Parole Authority opposing Glen's release, but he had been a model prisoner. He had completed all his therapeutic programs, he had avoided getting prison tattoos, he'd helped new inmates, he'd studied and received his teaching qualifications. He was coming out of jail and there was nothing the family could do.

Two months before his release date, Debbie met with Glen in prison. It was part of a Restorative Justice conference where offenders and victims meet and talk about what has happened. Her family couldn't understand why she needed to see him. They worried it would make things worse. But in the end her mother, sister and husband came with her. The Restorative Justice people had asked her: 'What *don't* you want from this conference?' Debbie had told them, 'I don't want Glen to say he is sorry.' She didn't want to hear this because it minimised Michael's murder. If he said sorry, she would not have believed him. And if she *did* believe him, that would have made him human, and she didn't want that either.

They walked into the room in the prison and sat down. Glen sat opposite Debbie. He had a nun with him, and Debbie noticed he was wearing an Our Lady medallion. She thought to herself, *Oh God, you've found God in prison.* Glen spoke, maintaining that Michael's death was an accident. Debbie asked the nun: 'Do you believe him?'; the nun replied, 'I believe he believes what he is saying is true.' Debbie showed Glen a photo of Michael's headstone and told him what he had done to her and her family.

'I gave Glen back the life he had given me,' Debbie told me. 'I gave him all my pain, my anger, my hatred and my fear. I left it all with him. I might sound cruel, but it gave me some peace to watch him, the movement of his body as I spoke to him, how he crumbled, and to know he was genuinely sorry he had killed his best mate. It was so important to me for him to realise what he had done to my children and me. Between walking into the conference and walking out, the change for me was instant. I felt it. I had given him all my suffering.'

Debbie had been a volunteer for the Homicide Victims' Support Group for twelve years and was now at university studying social work. She was in her mid-forties, she had just lost 23 kilos, and for the first time in her life she was asking herself: *Who am I? What do I want?*

She still often thought about Glen, but not in the way she once had. She used to believe in capital punishment. When Michael was murdered, she would have 'pushed the button' herself. But she was older and wiser now, and no longer knew if she supported the death penalty. How was someone's life worth more than someone else's? When Glen was released from prison, he joined the Salvation Army and began helping the homeless. When she learnt this she first thought, *I'll never donate to the Salvos again!* But then she thought, *Don't be stupid. He is doing something good. He's helping people.*

'I think that deep down Glen knows he murdered Michael,' she said. 'By being the model prisoner, and working for the Salvos, he is in some way saying he's remorseful.'

The voice recorder was flashing, and I went to turn it off when it occurred to me to ask her about Glen's soul.

'Where will Glen go once he dies?' I asked her.

She was silent.

'I honestly don't like to think that murderers go to the same place as we do,' she said finally. 'I don't think they deserve it: "Thou shalt not kill." But I also know that God forgives everybody. I struggle with this. We're taught as Catholics that if you go to confession and confess your sins . . . But I don't know. Can there be forgiveness for murder? Can there be forgiveness for kidnapping and killing a child? Can He forgive that evil? But then God is bigger than we are. I don't know. Maybe there *is* a hell that murderers go to. But then God forgives everybody, so that means everybody goes to heaven. I'm hoping Glen doesn't go to the same place as me. I'm hoping that God has little sections.'

Slowly, shyly, she began mapping out a tiered spatial logic of heaven: 'I think that really bad people have to go somewhere,' she said, flattening her palm out in front of her; 'other people here', raising her palm slightly; 'and us good people here', she said, stretching her hand above her head.

*

I sat on the edge of the bed where Jemima slept, synchronising my breathing with the little rise and fall of her chest. It was eleven o'clock. From the street, teenage voices singing a Taylor Swift song drifted up and into the night.

What had I expected of the day? Accounts of transcendence? Of spiritual solace and God's good grace? Of *forgiveness*?

I went to the kitchenette for a glass of water. The streetlight through the venetian blinds projected a silvery cage on the wall.

Something the man had said during the support group meeting was gnawing at me. He had asked me whose remorse I was interested in. *His* remorse, or his son's killer's? *He* felt remorse, he told me. What if he'd raised his boy differently? What if he'd done something differently? Maybe things would be different? Everyone else had felt the same, as if they could have somehow intervened in events, as if they could have prevented the killings.

I wondered if this was an effect of grief's uselessness. You can do nothing with grief but wait it out, let it do its slow work. If, on the other hand, you convince yourself you are feeling 'remorse' not 'grief', you claw back agency. Remorse demands action. A person can and must do something with it. Remorse can usher in healing, redemption, release.

Midnight. The wind whipped up, forcing the rain at angles.

I heard an irregular dripping sound, like a leaky tap. I crept into the bathroom, but found nothing. The drip pulsed for two, three, four, sometimes six beats and then paused just long enough to make me think it had ceased, before resuming. Where was it coming from? I opened the front door and stepped onto the landing. *Drip drip.* The noise was electrical, probably caused by a generator of some sort. I imagined it as an audio lighthouse beacon sending out calls to sightless ships.

Drip drip drip drip.

A dog barked somewhere in the distance.

Drip drip drip.

So much listening.

Night after night I listened out for Jemima's every peep, which meant I heard noises near and far. Sometimes I wished to be deaf. In the dark, bleak hours, I ached to be entirely senseless – a spirit stripped of sight, smell, taste, hearing, touch – so that I might harness rest. Every evening for years I'd used earplugs and an eye mask. I'd imagined myself in a cave. But I hadn't been able to block out sound.

Drip drip drip in the Wagga night.

A story resurfaced – one I'd hoped never would. I had read the news report at the very start of the remorse project when I was sleepless and half-crazed and desperate for deafness.

There is a mother from Perth, Western Australia. Her husband works in the mines, and she feels isolated; the couple have two young sons – a two-year-old and a ten-month-old – and the older boy is an erratic sleeper, he wakes his baby brother in the night, and the mother is exhausted, anaemic and depressed.

At two o'clock one afternoon she puts the boys in the shower, leaves the room to get soap, and lies down for just a moment. When she wakes ten hours later, she sees water at her feet. Somehow she hadn't heard the running shower, or the bathroom fan, or her boys: she had shut out the world's acoustics.

She rushes to the flooded bathroom and finds her children dead. She hysterically tries to revive them. 'Kill me, kill me, kill me!' she tells paramedics when they arrive.

IV

REHABILITATION

21

Years ago, when Brad and I moved into the apartment by the sea, we stood at the windows and stared out. We watched the thick strip of ocean, meringue peaks striking the base of the southern headland, and the great blue sky. As the months passed, I approached the glass less and less. The outlook was spectacular, but our living flouted gravity. There was an audacity about such views. We were floating so high, we could see so much; any moment the spell might be broken and we'd crash to earth.

Now we were in a house burrowed in a valley. Instead of looking down onto life, we looked up at our neighbours' homes, up at telegraph poles, up at tall, tall trees. It was a child's viewpoint, devoid of elevation and perspective.

I was back in the hurly-burly of the teaching semester. We'd returned from Wagga four weeks earlier. I'd placed my field notes in a corner of the study, unable and unwilling to look at them.

The rain came, great sheets billowing out from the gutters and eaves. We slunk around the house, heads cocked back, eyes prowling the ceiling. A leak was only a matter of time, and sure enough we found a steady drip in the lounge room, which became a *thwack* once we shoved a plastic bin under it. *Thwack! Thwack!* Then, when the water in the bin rose, *plop, plop, plop*.

We listened to the trampling rain throughout the days, and especially the nights.

After riding out a fallow period, Brad was now inundated with directing jobs. He was always on a film set somewhere, either in a studio or on location, which meant fifteen-hour days. When he was at home he'd hole himself up in the study writing directorial treatments for upcoming shoots. His bulging schedule restored his self-esteem, and our finances. But it also meant I saw him even less. Many times he'd be climbing into bed at 3 am just as I was getting up to start my working day. We'd pad past one another in the hallway, our fingertips grazing. I wondered if there would ever come a night when all three of us in the house slept at the same time.

One morning before dawn, I felt myself detaching from my marriage. An image appeared: Jemima and me living alone in an apartment together. It was disturbing the ease with which this picture settled in my mind. I'd always supposed it would be Brad who'd be the one to leave. But, no, it had been me who'd been making moves to go. Not in any practical sense, but through inaction. I'd stood by feebly as whatever had been holding us together dropped away.

*

Detaching from a loved one can result in detaching from others.

I would be with Jemima in the car, at the shops, at home, my mind elsewhere. She'd be right next to me while I rehearsed injurious exchanges with Brad, or assembled my future without him. Moments disintegrated. She'd be telling me something:

'Mum. Mummy! Mummee!!'

'What?!' I'd snap. 'What *is* it?'

She began saying sorry. She said it when I insisted she have a bath, or tidy her bedroom or go to sleep.

'Sor*reee*!!'

The sorrys multiplied. I'd be rushing to get dressed for work, and she'd say sorry. I'd be annoyed about the traffic, and she'd say sorry. Didn't sorry make everything better? Wouldn't it call her mother's spirit back into her body?

One evening she and I arrived home from the shops. She was pestering me but I was unpacking the eggs, ensuring none had cracked. She wandered off. I assumed she'd gone to her room to play. When dinner was ready I called out to her but there was no reply. I searched the house and the garden, my calls growing louder, more urgent. In the drizzle, I ran down the road to the park and there she was alone in the twilight, sitting on the damp swing, her little feet dangling above the dirt.

I had been unwilling to revisit the field notes from Wagga because they contained nothing but pain; and to revisit them would mean thinking about the case of that woman from Perth. A person judges herself for what she has done, and for what she's capable of doing. The story of that Perth woman was a sort of parable, its denouement a mother's most basic dread: what might happen if you turn your eyes and ears away from your children; what might happen if you drift to a place where you cannot be reached.

My husband and I were incapable of repairing our relationship by ourselves. Without consulting him, I phoned a couples' counselling service and booked the first available appointment.

Late one afternoon the rain let up. Brad was in the backyard, a stick in his hand, performing a sort of Tai Chi movement. He was relocating spiders, freeing up garden paths by lifting one end of sticky threads and placing them delicately on branches so they might re-attach themselves. From where I was watching, though, I couldn't see the webs. It looked as if he was stalking ghosts.

22

When I did finally recover my Wagga notes from a pile of paper, and when I sat down to read them, I saw that there was an abject starkness to the dialogue and descriptions. As far as victims' families were concerned, there was no place for an offender's remorse. There was simply no room for it – certainly not in this life, at least.

The Homicide Victims' Support Group had been co-founded by the parents of a Sydney nurse. The young woman had been abducted, raped and murdered in 1986. The five men responsible were serving life imprisonment. In an interview, the woman's father had spoken about his daughter's killers: 'I have learnt forgiveness, not for all of them, but for some of them. Not themselves physically, but their souls because they have to come to a more stern judgment than I could ever hope to have brought against them. But they will face it. And they will have to face it. And they'll have to be honest and say, "Yes, I did this thing." And then somebody will say, "God forgive their souls."'

'Somebody' will say.

At whose feet did judgment lie?

I tidied away the kitchen plates. Then I swept the floors and did a load of washing.

At whose feet did judgment lie?

I remembered something from the Bible that my father had muttered upon reading about yet another Catholic priest found guilty of sexually abusing children. In confessing to the Lord, the priest had considered himself absolved, as if he bore no civic responsibility, and that he and society were now square. 'Render unto Caesar the things that are Caesar's, and unto God the things that are God's,' Dad had said.

I sat down again with the field notes.

The Homicide Victims' Support Group members, like the rest of the community, wanted justice. And yet, in discussing the court cases of their dead family members, every one of them had spoken of 'our sentence', 'our conviction', as if they somehow owned the conflict. Deep down, though, they knew they *didn't* own it. They knew that vengeance was not theirs to mete out. The legal principle was crisp: technically, a crime is not committed against an individual; it is committed against the state. Unlike the civil courts, the criminal courts don't set plaintiff against defendant. It's offender versus the state. Immediately I thought of those two young men on death row in the Balinese prison, and of their parents being devoured by grief.

I put the pages aside.

In travelling to Wagga, in leading my family there, I had asked the wrong question. A study of remorse in the justice system demanded a different fearless probing.

The moral question was not what I would do if someone I loved fell victim to a horrid crime. The moral question was what I'd do if they committed one.

*

Samuel Connor had killed three friends in a car accident. He'd violated his parole order by drinking at the pub. Now the Authority had ordered him to appear before them to explain himself. Connor lived in an inland country town not far from Wagga. His trip to Sydney would take the best part of a day.

On the morning of Connor's parole hearing, I arrived at the Justice Precinct in Parramatta to find a twenty-person film crew outside the Sydney West Trial Courts. They were filming *Crownies*, an ABC TV legal drama. The actors were tanned and trim, nothing like the real people who frequent the courts, and when a handsome 'solicitor' turned his back to me, I saw comically large safety pins bunching together folds of suit fabric. The costume didn't fit him and this was wardrobe's shortcut.

Upstairs from the make-believe, three men stood in the public seating section at the back of Courtroom 4.07. It was Connor, with his father and his lawyer.

Tap tap. 'All rise.' Five Parole Authority members filed in, sat at the judge's bench and surveyed the room. Connor had refused to sit next to his dad and was slumped behind him as the lawyer sat up front in a comfy swivel chair. Connor was clean-shaven with polished shoes and tattoos. His hair, doubtless bushy when dry, had been firmly slicked down. His father was wan and weather-beaten, wearing old jeans that sat low on his hips. He rested his sunnies, cigarettes and a lighter on the bench in front of him.

Connor was called to sit next to his lawyer. Community Offender Services was now seeking more than another warning; it wanted a revocation. Connor was caught at the pub again last week. Community Offender Services wanted to send him back to prison.

Ian Pike explained to the lawyer: 'I must tell you, it's not looking good for your client.'

'I'm trying to convince my client that parole is mostly in the interest of the public, not the parolee,' the man said.

Pike commenced by calling Connor to give evidence. Connor dragged himself to the witness box, omitted 'Almighty God' by taking an affirmation rather than an oath, and sat. Slouching, he lifted his head to answer the lawyer's questions, most of which required 'yes' or 'no' answers. We learnt that he was twenty-seven and that he worked at the local mines.

'Your mother passed away two years ago, of cancer?' asked the lawyer.

'Yes,' replied Connor. He began to sob. He grabbed tissues and someone got him a glass of water. 'Mate, there's a lot of regrets there,' he croaked. His father rushed from the room.

Connor swallowed the tears and continued. His dad returned to his seat. We learnt that the father was a pensioner, that they lived together, and that in his town people worked and people drank: if Connor wanted friendships he had to go to the pub. We learnt that he once had a serious drug and alcohol problem, but that he had not used drugs since being in jail.

The lawyer explained to Connor that he must respect the fact that locals were still grieving.

'I *do*, mate. It's something I gotta live with for the rest of me life.'

The lawyer asked him if there was anything else he wished to say about his behaviour on parole.

'At times, I'm easily led. I should think more before I act. I've stuffed up and I've got to deal with the consequences,' came the reply.

It was the Parole Authority's turn. Some were moist-eyed. This man, they realised, wasn't petulant. He was grief-stricken. Pike gently talked to him about alcoholism, that it is a disease that can and should be treated, and about not socialising at the pub.

'Isn't this a small price to pay for reparation to the community for the crime you committed?'

Connor agreed: 'You don't have to explain to someone that they've done the wrong thing and killed three of their mates in a car accident. There might be some people that shrug it off, but —'

'We have not the slightest doubt that you feel it very much, but it is a fact and it can't be wiped out,' said Pike.

'No, it can't,' said Connor quietly.

Someone asked Connor whether he could remember what happened the night his friends were killed. He was crying. He said that his memory was muddled and that he had bad dreams.

A female Authority member asked if he was receiving counselling.

He said, 'Everything revolves around work. It's just get up, get to the mine and get fed.'

She told him that there were two things in his favour: his ongoing employment and his father's support. Connor sobbed harder at the mention of his dad.

Asked if he thought he had an alcohol problem, Connor said his idea of an alcoholic was a person who 'wakes up and cracks one'.

'My problem is that I think I'm dealing with things, and then I'm not,' he said. 'Where I come from, you are just an effing goose on the piss, if you know what I mean. Blokes say, "He's an effing goose on the piss."'

Connor could leave the stand. The Parole Authority heard from Connor's parole officer before leaving the courtroom to deliberate. Fifteen minutes later they were back. If parole were revoked, Connor would return to jail for twelve months before he could apply for release again. Pike asked him to stand, and took ten minutes to read the board's decision aloud. He announced, 'It is clear . . . that Mr Connor feels very deeply about the harm he caused to his friends and to the public by the commission of such serious offences.' Then to Connor: 'We feel compassion for you for the recent loss of your mother.' Connor couldn't stop crying. Pike continued: 'We hope there has been something of a breakthrough in your thinking today.'

They were not going to revoke parole. Instead, the Authority would make Connor attend Alcoholics Anonymous meetings and grief counselling. And then, by way of absolution, Pike said to him:

'You're a *young man*. You're entitled to be *much happier* than you are today.'

Outside the courtroom, Connor was flush-faced. There were no hugs or handshakes, just male mumblings drenched with relief. They made their way downstairs to the glass doors and stepped into the sunlight. The lawyer slipped on a Panama. Dad and son lit cigarettes. Huddled together, the three men walked slowly across the makeshift film set, past actor-cops in smooth costumes, and they stayed close and tight for as far as I could see them.

23

After Samuel Connor's hearing, I felt buoyant, as if just having watched a well-made play.

This perfect script found its way into my family life. One night, Jemima gave herself a bath, tidied her room and put herself to bed before I read her a book. Brad arrived home with a bunch of daffodils for me, the sunny blooms a symbol of truce and loyalty. Our impending counselling appointment was having the unexpected effect of unifying us, the way that quarrelling children clumsily unite when due to face the adult. I arranged the flowers in a vase on my desk and took deep pleasure in them as I worked.

Our counsellor was a Scottish guy about my age, who looked like a stand-up comedian, but who greeted Brad and me in the waiting area with a sincere expression. When we three entered his office and took our seats, which were arranged in a triangle, I instantly felt a structure grow, for here we had a non-judging third position. As Brad and I talked in that room, our partnership, which for too long had felt insubstantial, gradually altered its dimensions, becoming something solid and real onto which my husband and I could scramble.

I listened as Brad spoke of how much he loved Jemima and me, how he wanted to continue being a family; how, as a father and husband, he felt inconsequential, role-less, and at the same time, although his wife earned a decent salary, he felt burdened by being The Provider, frightened about what it meant for the future and for his filmmaking. Then Brad listened as I too spoke about my frustrations and fears, my desire for deep connection with him and my need for on-the-ground support. The counsellor commented on how much love and respect there was between us, and that he was partly wondering why we'd come to the session at all, because, if we simply communicated as we had done here and now, then the conflict we were having at home could be easily resolved. I was pleased to hear this, although I felt like a hypochondriac: I'd rushed us to the doctor over nothing. Then again, it had taken this appointment to get Brad to talk the way he had.

My husband and I left the session hand-in-hand. We agreed that it had been an important sixty minutes, and that we were definitely willing to change: he would be more open with me, he'd rein in his anger and he'd shoulder more of the domestic load; I would be less scrutinising, less sensitive, curbing my unrealistic expectations of him and of myself. It felt straightforward, as if the culprit of our marital woes had been a dislocated joint that was now popped back into place.

That night the three of us ate takeaway pizza, and we played Charades, Jemima's rendition of a flamingo leaving us doubled-over with laughter. Then we turned off all the lights, crept outside and lay on our backs together on the shabby toddler trampoline, three astronomers beneath the fluttering stars.

*

I was so enthralled by the episode with Samuel Connor, its impact on me having increased even further due to the ebullient mood in which I found myself after the counselling appointment, that I decided to relay it to my friend Ruth, the former defence lawyer, who years earlier had followed the case of the woman who'd run over the young man, killing him.

At the Parole Authority offices the previous day, I had asked Ian Pike about Connor's case, and whether his testimony in the witness box had affected the board's decision. 'Yes, I'm sure it did,' Pike said. 'It was part of the whole thing. I come from the country. I know his type of young man, brought up to be tough, insensitive, not to show emotion, probably never hugged his parents in his life. But he did start breaking through and that had a very powerful effect on the board. In that matter, it was clear he was feeling remorse in a genuine, human way.' Then Pike began to weep. He spoke of Connor's 'metamorphosis' in court, and that 'during that hour of the inquiry, it was as if all matters fell away and this matter became the entire reason for the board's existence'.

But when I recounted all this to Ruth over lunch, she was unmoved.

'It's all well and good that the board heard directly from this kid in person, and that it seemed to work out okay for him, but how about all the other poor buggers who are forced to use the AV-link to plead their cases?' she said. 'It's impossible to have a human conversation via that thing. And the stakes are so *high*. If a guy's parole is revoked, he has to remain in prison for an entire twelve months before he can apply for re-release! It's completely unjust.'

A waiter took our order. I was grateful for the interruption. I agreed with Ruth, having also reached this conclusion about the audiovisual link, but for once I wanted her to suspend her critique and surrender to a heartwarming story.

Instead, I changed the subject. I told her about my car accident and the negligent driving ticket, certain she would help me find humour in the ordeal.

Her face scrunched.

'Oh Kate, you don't want a neg driving conviction on your record.'

'But the policeman said it wasn't a criminal offence. That it was more like a speeding ticket.'

'No it's not!' she said. 'I hate it when the police give out summary justice! There are grey areas. For example, having an apprehended violence order put out against you isn't a criminal offence, but you don't want it either. Neg driving is also in that grey area. Can you appeal it? What evidence did they have against you? Just because you went up someone's bum doesn't mean it's neg driving.'

I explained that I'd voluntarily gone to the police and made a statement about how I'd crashed into Rob's car. Ruth was dumbstruck. Seeing the look on her face, I felt like a halfwit.

'*Never* make a statement to the police!' she said. 'Say nothing! What were you thinking?'

'I wanted to tell the truth.'

'There *is* no truth! In the justice system there is no truth! It's about interpretation. If you hadn't given that statement, the police wouldn't have been able to convict you. The onus of proof is on *them*. Let them prove it.'

I fiddled with my rocket salad. I thought back to something David had said all those years ago: *There's being honest, and there's being stupid.*

'Why don't you appeal it anyway?' she continued. 'Get the statement you made to the police and show it to me, and I'll tell you if you've got a chance. If I were you, I'd go to court. The problem with having a neg driving conviction is that if you ever have another driving mishap it won't look good.'

'I can't go before the magistrate and appeal. It's morally wrong. The fact is I *did* glance away from the road before the prang.'

'There's a difference between being morally wrong and being legally wrong. Our system is such that the police have to prove you were *legally* wrong.'

'Morally I can't do it,' I told her. 'Anyway, I'd be terrified to go to court. And I don't want to waste the court's time.'

'You're an ethnographer. You'd love it!'

I walked up the steep hill to my car.

Perhaps the label 'negligent driving' wasn't meant to describe my action of accidentally banging into the back of a car in traffic. Perhaps it was meant for other types of cockeyed conduct.

Legal evidence gets stitched together to form a history. It's not about what happened, it's what the police can *prove* happened beyond reasonable doubt. While Christianity assumes we're all sinners, the justice system presumes us innocent until found guilty; and yet, by voluntarily walking into that police station and confessing, I'd confused structures. Perhaps, in the law, conscience had no role – in which case I should have just swapped insurance details with Rob; or, if the police had to be involved, I should have stayed quiet and procured a lawyer, who would have stared down the cops and demanded they produce evidence against me. Ruth was right. Perhaps my accident wasn't negligent driving. Perhaps the police hadn't proved it was negligent driving. Yes, I looked away from the road and smacked into Rob's car, but perhaps I was legally innocent.

When I got home I phoned the External Information Access & Subpoena Unit and was emailed two application forms – one to obtain my statement, the other to obtain the relevant police incident report – that I was to complete and lodge with a $109 fee.

24

Physicists don't talk in terms of time. They prefer to think of distance, light years, the relationship between objects. Time is an abstraction, they tell us. We observe shifts in our world – the sun rising and setting, rain falling, plants flowering, people growing old and dying – and we use the concept of time to label moments in the universe. It is about observable change: we perceive objects in some particular arrangement, and then in another arrangement, and we use 'time' to measure the interval between configurations.

I lay in the spare bed. It had been eight weeks since the counselling appointment. I could not tell if my marriage was improving. I'd tried returning to our bedroom, but Brad's snoring had left me tense. Each day I was on alert for signs that our home life was different, our union restored. He'd written me a beautiful card for my birthday, accompanied by a selection of new books. He'd helped me with an extensive data transfer from my old laptop to my new one. He'd unpacked the dishwasher more often. But we'd had altercations too.

In describing the journey of our marriage, I wanted to be able to use the term 'breakthrough' – 'We've had a breakthrough' – and to speak of 'then' and 'now', 'before' and 'after'.

The criminal courts were expert at identifying the 'before' and the 'after'. They were preoccupied with change. An event takes place. Something happens. Police arrive and gather evidence. The courts analyse the occurrence, its cause and effect, the person or persons responsible. Legal cases are forensic reconstructions of moments in time and space, mapping the different configurations. Then, afterwards, a person's sentence involves further rearrangement. One of the seven official purposes of sentencing in New South Wales is 'To promote the rehabilitation of the offender'. It is what the community hopes for: that people leave jail reformed.

I propped myself up in bed and grabbed the notebook that was sitting on the floor. The previous day I'd written the word 'transformation'. Truly contrite offenders changed their lifestyles, changed their ways.

For weeks I'd been visiting the Community Restorative Centre on Broadway in Chippendale. Housed in a 1933 art deco building that was once a bank, the government-funded organisation provided support services for prisoners, parolees and their families. It was a place where caseworkers assisted former inmates to make straight-and-narrow plans, helping them reshape their lives.

If personal change was the crux of the matter, then how was it measured, and who or what did the measuring? How many tiny moments of not-doing-what-you-might've-once-done must accrue to form an identifiable index of transformation?

I'd been accompanying a 31-year-old caseworker as she made house calls to her clients, men in their first twelve months out of jail. Many of them were still looking for employment, and had no family or friends, she'd told me. She worried about the men's 'use of time', how they'd impose structure on their days.

We visited a parolee who had spent his adulthood in and out of prison. He was plagued by dysfunction: drug and alcohol problems, heavy debt, a long history of abuse. He was in his forties and had been service-dependent all his life, raised in institutions since he was a toddler. The caseworker said that, when they were little, her clients were considered 'at risk'; then from eighteen upwards, they're considered 'a risk': people have compassion for them as they're growing up in horrible environments, but once they turn eighteen, there's no more empathy. These vulnerable clients were expected to make sound life decisions despite never having had a role model.

The man was temporarily living in a house owned by the Centre. We arrived out the front and the caseworker, willowy and unflappable in the way of netball goalies, slipped out of the car, plucked a whipper snipper from the back seat, and handed it to the man who'd come outside to greet us. We followed him into the house. At the end of a dark hallway was a sunny, blank-walled lounge room with a large window of sky. Apart from a couple of sofas and a coffee table, there was an old TV, two dozen DVDs, a heater and six bottles of Brut spray-can deodorant. There was also a single mattress on which lay a black-and-white striped doona and floral-patterned pillow. Later, the caseworker would tell me that the parolee slept in the lounge room because it made him feel safe. He had the sleeping habits of children 'in care', who'd learnt young to remain in a state of watchful alertness. Kids who kept their eyes on the front door.

She handed him a form – Housing Pathways – which he filled out painstakingly. He didn't know how much child support he was paying. His former partner and child lived in Tasmania. He had other kids elsewhere but he wouldn't say how many. As he printed answers in the little boxes, he kept wiping his forehead with his sleeve. He'd started wearing nicotine patches two days earlier and was waiting for them to kick in. He was studying an electrician course at TAFE three days a week, and was currently on a term break: a good time to give up smoking.

I told him I was researching how the justice system works, and he guffawed: 'You think the justice system works? Nah. Blokes who get a sentence of six months to two years don't have a chance.

At the prison farm, they treat you like children. When you get out, they give you a train ticket, half a dole cheque, a "Thanks for coming", and you're back on the street. If you get six months, you don't get visitors. You get a "Dear John" from the missus.'

We talked about prison, how he'd just spent five months inside for 'pissy larceny', and I asked him whether, with this latest conviction, the judge had reckoned he was sorry for stealing. 'Why should I be sorry?' he said. 'The only time you have to be sorry is if there's violence. Or a white-collar crime. You know, if there's a full-on victim. The stuff I deal with is brand new from the warehouse. If I wanna do you over, I wanna do it when you're not there.' The caseworker sat quietly. The man glanced at her, then me: 'It all goes back to drugs,' he announced, satisfied with his perspicacity. 'That's been my problem: drugs. Addressing drugs in jail? Fuggetaboutit.'

He wanted a smoke so we stepped outside where there was a pergola from which hung a cobweb-covered punching bag, and beyond the concrete paving was metre-high herbage that took up half the backyard. He liked the act of smoking, he said, inhaling, admitting that he was 'dirty on heroin', that sometimes he wanted 'that cold steel'. Heroin was a personal drug, he explained, while alcohol was a social drug. The problem with alcohol was that he could get violent. He was finding it hard to stay off heroin, especially living by himself with no one to talk to.

'Will you become friends with the other TAFE students?' I asked.

'They're all so straight. Naïve,' he said. 'The other day they were talking about how blue lights have been installed in the bathroom so people can't find their veins to shoot up. I laughed. You don't need to see your veins to shoot up!'

'What about finding friends at the pub?' the caseworker suggested.

'The pub. That was a joke.' Then to me: 'I was lonely. But I got barred from the pub! For talking to people. I was told: "People come to the pub to get pissed. Not to talk to people."'

No one said anything.

'What will you do for the rest of the week?' the caseworker finally asked him.

'Dunno. Check my Keno ticket.'

'You bought a ticket? Why did you do that?'

'I was bored. It's up to two point one million. It'd be a life-changer. You never know your luck in a big city.' He paused, considering the days ahead. 'I gotta go to Centrelink on Wednesday.'

'Come into the Centre for a coffee,' she told him. 'Something to do. An outing.'

No answer. Then, as if for the first time, he registered the small forest of vegetation leisurely nudging itself towards the house.

'I'll whipper-snip tomorrow.'

We said our goodbyes and left.

For isolated people, small talk with neighbours and other people in their community gives shape to formlessness, ensuring survival. But small talk for parolees was a struggle. Their entire lives were socially impolite to discuss.

In prison, the sort of talk the authorities encouraged was that which might tame the past event: an account of self-transformation. Months ago, I'd sat next to a chirpy parole officer in court. She worked in the jails. She'd told me how remorseless prisoners would come to her hoping to apply for release, and she'd repeatedly tell them: 'Go away, think about what you've done, and then come back and see me.'

Sometimes, this insistence that inmates put words to expired action had the effect of instilling in them a frenzied tale of conversion. At the Centre one day, I'd chatted with a 36-year-old Seventh-day Adventist Fijian-Australian woman. She was soft and bosomy and kept apologising to the Lord. Her sixteen trips to jail had mostly been for credit-card fraud. ('I was a credit-card fraudster. I'm so ashamed. Sorry, Lord.') She'd go to gym lockers 'searching, prowling, looking for a rip', and she'd nick credit cards from people's purses. Then she'd hire a suite at the Novotel and go shopping. She was a superior forger. Her mates would phone her: 'Hey, I've got a card! I'm in Bondi Junction! Get down here!' She'd jump in a cab and meet them in the shop. She'd discreetly sign the cardholder's signature in the air a couple of times before approaching the service counter and doing it for real. With each arrest she was caught red-handed. In court she'd always say sorry. Altogether she stole $365,000. In jail, she did the drug and alcohol therapeutic program Enough Is Enough, as well as Out of the Dark, a program aimed at domestic violence offenders and victims of domestic violence.

'My mentality was: I'm taking their cards, but I'm not hurting anybody,' she told me. 'You pay insurance. You get your money back. I'm not putting a needle to nobody's neck. I'm not smashing or snatching anyone. I now realise that I was hurting people.'

When she got out of prison a few months ago, she walked into the Centre 'with my little bag' and asked for help.

'This is my last chance at a good life,' she said. 'I'm not doing crime anymore. It's the end of the yellow brick road for me. I pray every night and ask God to forgive me.'

The woman's story was hyped-up, compressed – *I was blind, but now I see* – and she found herself peddling it to whoever would listen. It made her proud to tell it, even though she could not immediately recognise how the story might map onto her attempts to move forward in her life.

On the other hand, I'd interviewed parolees who were distressed by the narratives of themselves they'd been forced to tell. As part of a rehabilitation exercise in jail, some inmates had been made to write their own autobiographies. The psychologists were searching for people's 'core belief': why the offenders thought it'd all gone wrong. One man I spoke with produced a story of his life of poverty and how it led to crime: when he was young he saw his friends had material possessions that they'd stolen; he saw how easily they were getting the stuff and he wanted it too, so he began stealing, doing armed robbery. But the psychologists were unhappy with the man's account of himself. They told him that the reason he was in prison was that he didn't have a father figure and that he was unloved. The man was confused: he got on well with his family, he was close to them. His offending had nothing to do with love; it was that they were poor. His family had to scramble for food. They had nothing. But in order to satisfy the jail authorities, in order to demonstrate rehabilitation, he changed his story and told them: 'Okay, I was unloved.'

Transition was the breezy term authorities used to describe an inmate's re-entry to the outside world, the world of employment, stable housing, clean living.

'When have your clients transitioned? When can you use past tense?' I asked the caseworker.

'I don't think you ever can,' she said. 'Transition is an ongoing process.'

She was referring to the drudgework of penance. The term transition cloaked a daily labour that none of us wants to acknowledge, for no one likes to equate change with toil. Instead, we hunger for tales of remorse and absolution. We want to hear about elegant epiphanies in the selfish hope that restorative stories might act as prophylactics for our lives, allowing us to palliate what has gone before, and what has not yet happened, rescuing our families and ourselves all at once.

I placed the notebook back down on the floor beside me, turned over and eventually fell asleep.

The next morning Brad left early for work, kissing me so slightly that our lips barely touched. I couldn't tell if the half-heartedness of it was a small act of defiance.

In the paper I read the latest news report about Andrew Chan and Myuran Sukumaran, the two Australian men in Bali facing the death penalty. They were lodging an appeal with the Indonesian Supreme Court and were being represented by a top Melbourne barrister. They were receiving hate mail, which they accepted with equanimity for they thoroughly recognised the graveness of their acts, and yet still they couldn't quite believe that Indonesia wished them dead.

I read of their spectacular rehabilitation. In Kerobokan prison, Chan had turned to Christianity, he was leading the English-language church service, and, from what we were seeing in the reports, he sustained a relentless optimism that buoyed other detainees. 'God didn't put me in here. He allowed me being here so I can see Him,' he told an interviewer. 'He allowed things to happen, so that I might learn how to live.'

Sukumaran had also become a mentor, and was teaching classes to his fellow inmates in English, computer skills, graphic design and philosophy. He seemed quieter than Chan, more circumspect, and he had learnt to paint. In the prison workshop, he was surrounded by a garland of canvases; unforgiving self-portraits in blood hues, his face exposed to the light.

'The painter and the pastor', someone had dubbed the two men.

Their rehabilitation was absolute. Surely the state's revenge could be more modest. Surely their lives would be spared.

25

Jemima was asking questions about how her brain worked and how her heart beat, so Brad bought her a book, *See Inside Your Body*. It had more than fifty flaps designed for little fingers to pry open and point to vivid, blobby organs and twisting tubes. Jemima tittered at the rude illustrations in 'Eating and Excreting', and she puzzled over 'Brain Power' with its yellow amoeba-like renderings of neurons. But the section with which she was most taken showed off our skeleton and muscles. She stared at the hollow-eyed skull, she wanted to know what tendons and joints were, and how all that red stretchy stuff attached itself to bone. Slack-jawed, she asked us, 'So *this* is under my *skin*?'

When Jemima was much younger I'd wondered at what point she would become aware that she had an 'inside' and that it was hidden. As a baby, you ingest and expel stuff, but it's many months before you are conscious you're doing so, and before you connect your parents' explanations to your own experience ('Where's the pear gone? It's in your tummy!'; 'Let's change your nappy. Pee-eww!'). Jemima asked where she came from, and we told her that babies grew in mummies' bellies and that she'd grown in mine, and she peered up at my middle and wondered how she'd fitted. Her developing sense of insideness wasn't only anatomical. When she first began reporting her thoughts and dreams, she figured them as having formed outside her and floated into her head. When she was barely three years old, however, I encountered a very new, very different cognisance in her. I discovered crushed crayons, magnets, bit of wool and Lego strewn on the lounge room floor. 'Who made this mess?' I asked lightly, expecting her to proudly answer, 'Jemima!' like she'd always done. Not this time. 'Belle,' she said, her gaze challenging mine. Belle. She was blaming her little cousin who lived interstate. I smiled: Jemima had learnt how to lie. Suddenly she was aware of, and had control over, the layers of her presentation. Suddenly she had a secret self.

Now, almost two years later, she was adept at fibbing. She would casually announce that she'd eaten her carrot, or brushed her teeth, when she hadn't. The fibs were infrequent and for a while I'd found them amusing, a sign of intelligence. It was now becoming disconcerting. She had my artfulness at splitting: the fluent ability to suppress a certain response while completing a separate task, to balance more than one reality in her head. I worried it might become a habit. That I was two people was the result of growing up with my father. It is the cruel effect of anger: if you've been the target of someone's aggression, you never forget it; if you've lived with an angry parent, you will be forever fearful of them, forever presenting to them a studied comportment as a decoy. I did not want this division for my child. I wanted Jemima unconcealed, unified. I wanted to instil in my preschooler that basic human dictum: Know Thyself.

'Tell me the truth!' I demanded one morning.

'I am!' she insisted.

'Don't lie! There's no reason to lie. I won't be angry. Just tell me.'

'I am telling the truth!'

She watched me walk away, the ice from her mother spreading through the house.

The next day, I arranged to see Bob Inkster, the decorated police detective I'd sat next to during parole meetings. I wanted to talk with him about confessions, how police speak with wrongdoers, how they build pictures of what really happened.

At Bob's suggestion we met up at a café in a tidy brown shopping complex adjacent to a garden supply shop, in a suburb with one of the lowest crime rates in the country. He spoke about detective work; he said that one of the greatest weapons a detective can have is perception, which you can pick up only with experience. You go to a crime scene. You speak to witnesses. You must eliminate as much as you investigate. You have local knowledge about similar crimes in the area, you have intelligence from informants and from members of the public. You eventually come to a belief as to what most likely happened and how it happened; and then you work out who has committed the crime. Attention to detail is critical. You can't under-do a matter. Teamwork is not only the best way, it is the only way.

The art is to get people to talk to you and tell you the truth, Bob said. Communication is a major tool. Knowing people is invaluable. And yet nowadays police use audiovisual recordings when formally interviewing criminals, and this has reduced the professionalism of the interrogator because 'a lot of waffle goes into it – the interrogator doesn't have a plan'. In the old days, you would ask a question and your colleague would type down the question and then the offender would give an answer, which would be typed down too, and you'd have time to think of your next line. These days, however, interviewers aren't mindful of what has already transpired, and often they want to be the star of the show. In an interrogation, if you've got the answer you are looking for, don't ask another question on it. Keep to the point, otherwise everything gets clouded in rubbish. Knowing when to say nothing is a very valuable tool. You have to let the offender do most of the talking. Sometimes a very good question is, 'What happened then?'

When someone is trying to make something up, said Bob, they are invariably hesitant. But the truth pours out of people. And, when it comes to deciding on a person's remorse, you can see it, you can feel it and you can smell it. You can sense remorse in the actions of a person, their demeanour, the way they speak, the emotion in it. It's a gut feeling more than anything.

Bob headed inside to the counter to pay for our drinks.

I wanted to tell him about the nightmares I'd been having, variations of the same scene: in one, I'm driving when Jemima climbs out of her car seat and onto my lap and I mow down two men standing outside the Coogee Bay Hotel; in another, my foot can't find the brake and I plough into a pedestrian at an intersection on Epping Road. At the end of each dream, I sit rigid at the steering wheel while onlookers rush to the mangled bodies on the street.

'Bob,' I said when he returned. 'One last thing.'

I told him about my car accident, how I'd been convicted of negligent driving, and that Ruth had urged me to appeal it.

'Was it okay for the policeman to book me for negligent driving without him going to the accident scene? And was it even negligent driving at all?'

'He had no option,' Bob said bluntly. 'Any vehicle that has to get towed from an accident scene is mandatory reporting. In terms of it being negligent driving, you've got to have your eye on the vehicle in front, and be able to drive at a safe distance from them.'

'So, in reporting it, I did do the right thing?'

'You did, yeah.'

'But now I have a negligent driving conviction, which is serious.'

'On what you tell me, though, the degree of negligence was minimal. I wouldn't lose one more second of sleep over it. You are in the majority of people, not the minority. What you've done is minor.'

'But still it was classed as "negligent". It'll be on my record forever.'

'If you had taken it to court, and assuming you've got no prior convictions, it's unlikely you would've got a monetary penalty. Similarly, had you taken the option of making representations to the police department explaining exactly what you've told me, there's a chance they may have just given you a caution. But the officer who took the details didn't have that authority.'

'So do I have bugger-all chance of doing anything about it now?'

'You got a monetary fine and you paid it?'

'Yeah.'

'I think that you'd have bugger-all chance.' Then he looked me square in the eye and added: 'Anyway, Kate, from what you tell me, it's a prima facie case, you know?'

Half an hour later I was at home.

From my desk I retrieved the Request for Incident Report form, the one that would've helped me appeal my conviction. I screwed it up and chucked it in the bin.

Later, as I collected Jemima from preschool, she said: 'Mummy, from now on I will tell the truth. I don't want you to be angry.'

'I'm not angry, sweetheart.'

'Yes you were. You were angry yesterday.'

'No I wasn't, was I?'

'Yes. You were mean.'

'Really?'

'Yes.'

I didn't know what to say.

'Let's buy some ice cream,' I suggested.

She and I sat in the park eating Paddle Pops, watching kids swing themselves from one end of the monkey bars to the other.

Raimond Gaita once referred to remorse as 'a disciplined remembrance of the moral significance of what we did'. It takes discipline to reconcile who you think you are with what you've done.

Not long ago I'd spoken with a top state public defender about his experience of defending murderers. He said that straight after the killing, often the person denies responsibility because they have enormous difficulty accepting mentally what they have just done. Most people who commit murder have never before committed any sort of crime; the act that causes the death is an explosion in their brain of anger and frustration that is unprecedented, and they discover, to their horror, that they're holding this bloodied knife. They are in utter disbelief, and they quite genuinely believe that they couldn't have done it, that someone else has come in and done it. The evidence has to be put before them so they can begin to accept what happened. Sometimes, it's as if the trial isn't there to convince the court about the offender's guilt; the trial is there to prove to the offender she did it.

*

I came down with a cold, a headache attaching itself vice-like to my skull.

Re-morse, re-habilitation, re-sentment, re-concile. All those 're-'s, like nervous tics. Philosophers called remorse a 'retractive' emotion; it involved a person retreating or resiling from his action or state of being.

Brad and I had said that we were both willing to change, but talking about change doesn't make it so. My despair was thorough. I couldn't see a cure for us. Perhaps we were over. Jemima was almost five years old. She would be starting school next year. *Please, God, don't let this ruin her life.*

I hunted for pain relief tablets at the bottom of my handbag, and salvaged a flattened Disprin packet. One tab left.

My parents used to keep the family's medicine in a container on a high shelf in the yellow kitchen cupboard. My father would be irritated if he reached for the Disprin and the packet was empty; indeed, whenever supplies ran out and we hadn't alerted The Household: milk cartons, bread sleeves, cracker boxes, Vegemite jars, butter tubs, sticky-tape rolls, detergent bottles, staples packs. I learnt never to use the last of anything. Nothing was ever finished. There was always a scrap of loo paper, juice dregs, a tea bag, three staples, a single Disprin safe inside its silver square.

I ripped open the foil, plopped the disc in water, and watched it dissolve.

It is said that life is short, but it is also very long, meaning it is possible for us to live a thousand different lives. A decade ago when he retired from the university, my father completely transformed. It stupefied my siblings and me. The metamorphosis felt mythic. Within months of leaving work, he developed a rare skin condition, red and swollen and unbearably itchy, that dermatologists diagnosed as an autoimmune disorder, *pityriasis rubra pilaris*: 'red pillar'. There was no known cure.

Having devoted his career to the study of science, Dad was now its object. His skin turned scaly, callused, encasing him. His hands and feet were especially besieged, and when his soles began to split, he couldn't walk. Not all of his body was affected; there were patches of skin that remained free from the disease, doctors referring to them as 'islands of sparing'. Each time I saw him he looked redder and redder, consumed by a fire from the inside out. It was distressing to watch him suffer, and I spoke with my brother, who had expertise in anatomy and physiology, of what could be done to save him. Other, far less exalted feelings came to me. Try as I might to stuff it down, a springy, unsayable word stuck in my throat: *comeuppance*.

As the crust thickened, Dad disappeared further into himself, and my mother wondered if she might lose him altogether. A doctor took a chance and issued a drug not usually prescribed for such a thing. At first it didn't work but then Dad's skin gradually began to clear, becoming less and less lobster-like. The hard parts cleaved off. My father emerged changed.

I can accept now that that's what happened – he changed profoundly, or as Mum saw it, the side of her husband she'd always known was there expressed itself consistently and unreservedly – but I was not certain I could really trust it. When he suddenly began behaving so gently, so full of love, when he told me how precious I was, I kept waiting for the old habit to reassert itself. The moments of change had to accrue before I could use the verb 'transformed', for a person's transformation is a sort of riddle that only makes itself apparent after the fact. I was still adjusting to this wise, adoring father. I did not know what to do with the husk of the past. Around him I did not know how to shake off my armoured self.

Arriving at my parents' house that afternoon, I heard singing and recognised the tune. Dad was teaching Jemima an old German folk song, one that he'd sung to us when we were little.

Marmalada, Kaffalada, Eisbär Schnitzel, un Blumenkohlsalat
Un sour Gherkin, Un Wasser Coco, Unta Hafaschlass
Hunger, Hunger, Hunger, Hunger

The song sounded completely made-up, with its silly language and *oom-pah* beat, but it wasn't. Viennese children had sung it after the war, and this was Dad's mishmashed recollection of it. Marmalade. Polar bear schnitzel. Cauliflower salad. Sour gherkin. Cocoa made with water. Slimy oats. Hunger.

Jemima was enchanted. 'Polar bear schnitzel, Mum! Papa's singing about *polar bear schnitzel*!'

My mother was at an appointment but had made a pot of chicken soup, which Dad helped me secure in the front passenger seat of my car.

He kissed my forehead.

'You and I should have a coffee soon,' I told him.

He nodded, although I knew he was taken aback. We never sat down together alone, just the two of us.

As Jemima and I drove away, she strained to wave goodbye through the rear window, her papa growing smaller and smaller as the street, the cars, the trees and the sky fanned out around him.

26

The minister at the Uniting Church my parents attend has a doctorate in theoretical physics from Oxford University. It seems an anomaly that scientists, for whom the building of knowledge based on empirical evidence is fundamental, are often absorbed by the metaphysics of Being, Existence and Time. But according to the minister, it is possible to accommodate both the insights of science and the wisdom of Biblical narrative. Maths is, after all, the language of the cosmos.

In his homilies, he has talked about the creation story, how in the Bible the Hebrew poet wrote that in the beginning 'the earth was a formless void and darkness covered the face of the deep'. The poet was not saying that God created everything *ex nihilo*, out of nothing; he was not foreshadowing modern cosmology's concept: 'before the big bang'. According to the minister, the story is telling us that when God began his creating, the earth (that was formless) and the deep (the oceans) were already there. Jewish cosmology hated chaos, the minister says. Ancient Hebrews saw entropy as the enemy of the work of a God of order and structure; according to them, the formless void, the water, the chaos were there as raw materials for the Spirit of God to work upon and make meaningful. The minister also quotes a Hasidic saying that each of us should carry around two pieces of paper, one in each pocket. When we are feeling proud and self-important we should read the words: 'I am but dust and ashes.' When we are feeling worthless and ashamed, we read: 'For me the world was created.' These things are both true and untrue. We are somewhere in between.

My father's belief that we exist in this in-betweenness, at the limits of what is knowable and explainable, at the boundary of spirit and flesh, was what helped him to heal and transform. Soon after the illness cleared, he noticed that the date in August 2003 when his skin condition had first appeared was exactly the same day half a century earlier that his ten-year-old self had left Austria. The drug the doctor prescribed had certainly helped to relieve the suffering, but Dad sensed that something beyond the material realm was also at play.

Cosmologists say that the further we look into space, the further back in time we go, for when we look at objects long distances away, the light we see was emitted from those objects many years earlier. Perceiving the past takes time. Memoirists know this too. Memoirists know, for instance, that is it easier to write about a parent once he is dead, the extinguished life leaving behind traces for the observing daughter to make of them what she will. My father was still alive, he lived a twenty-minute drive from me, and yet I did not know how to begin an intimate conversation with him. I could, of course, bypass him altogether. If information about his family was what I wanted, I could go to Vienna, seek out archives, compile lists of dates and places and employment, a dossier of who-did-what-when. But I love my dad. There are doors he is not ready to open, which means I shan't open them either. Not yet. And, anyway, information isn't story. What use is a battery of historical facts?

When I was twenty-four, I wrote Dad a letter. This was before his illness, before he'd changed. I had been seeing a psychologist in an attempt to disrupt a cycle of unhealthy relationships. Since my mid-teens, I'd been doing what girls in my position did – girls who'd abandoned hope of a proper paternal relationship – which was to court boyfriends much older than me, grown men who should have known better. The psychologist had suggested I write to my father, so I did. I poured out my heart, telling him how hurt I felt, and how much I loved him. I sent it off and waited. After a week, when I'd heard nothing, I phoned him.

'Did you get my letter, Dad?'

'Yes.'

Silence.

'Do you have a response to it?' I asked. 'To what I wrote?'

'It's a shame you feel that way about things.'

We each hung up the phone.

It was now a decade and a half later. A child never stops trying to reach out to a parent, and there is more than one way to write to someone.

*

After midnight one night on the prison island of Nusakambangan in Indonesia, Andrew Chan and Myuran Sukumaran were led outside with six other inmates to a jungle clearing, where a white apron was draped over each of them, a red target across their hearts. The group sang 'Amazing Grace' before being shot dead.

In the weeks, days, hours leading up to Chan's and Sukumaran's executions, the Australian government, Christian leaders and imams had pleaded for clemency, with more than 150,000 people signing a petition: *spare their lives, give the men a second chance.*

Wasn't redemption supposed to be met with mercy?

The story we were hoping for had been cut short. The script had gone awry.

27

My father made us both a coffee and we sat in my parents' backyard admiring the young olive trees. He knew about my research, how the presence of remorse in the courts was a theological hangover from previous centuries. I had told him I wanted to speak with him about his relationship with Christianity, which was true, and had asked would he mind if I recorded the conversation.

When did he first become involved in the church? It was a biographer's question, the elementary sort a daughter can ask her father.

'My memories are not strong,' he said. He told me about being five years old and being on a summer camp in the Austrian countryside and learning folk songs. He was taken to a church with thirty other children, and the church was dark, and he felt something spiritual. It was a comfortable presence, he felt he belonged, that he'd come home, and much later, on the other side of the world, he would call this feeling 'God'. This was when he was living at the hostel in Sydney, with the Methodist minister and his wife, both joyful people, he said, and he was 'in a cloud of spiritual Christian consciousness'.

When Dad reads and reflects on the scriptures nowadays, he tries to engage beyond the words: their cultural overlay, the fact that they are gateways rather than stopping points. Theologian Marcus Borg says language about God must be metaphorical, that 'metaphors are intrinsically nonliteral. A metaphor affirms, even as it also implicitly denies: x is y, x is not y.' Dad is drawn to three stories in the Jewish history. Exodus: God saves, He frees you from Egypt, from bondage. Exile: God brings you back from a place where God is not, to a place where God is. And the Priestly Story, 'which is about sacrifice, the cleansing of sin through sacrifice – but you have to prepare first before the sacrificial act can take place; you have to rid yourself of disharmony'.

He told me about his strange skin condition, how unendurably itchy it was, how he'd covered himself in sorbolene cream, how he'd been awake every night and tried to relieve it by showering. After six months he was desperate. He sensed that the cause of the disease was not only physical but psychic too. He went to an old friend, Canon Jim Glennon, founder of a well-known healing ministry in Sydney. The scripture says: 'Are any among you sick? They should call for the elders of the church . . . The prayer of faith will save the sick, and the Lord will raise them up.' Dad thought to himself, *Okay, I will do this*. He told Jim: 'You are my elder. Do your stuff.'

Dad started attending Jim's weekly church healing service, one that also emphasised healing as a journey, a way of life. And, at night, Dad began reviewing his life. Memories came to him about people he had hurt and disappointed. He asked for that person to forgive him, and he asked God to heal that person. Whether the person was dead or alive, it did not matter. This process went on for an extended time, and he arrived at a belief that such healing was possible.

'Did you phone people and apologise?'

'No, I didn't necessarily need to find the person and say sorry,' he said. 'Sometimes it is the last thing that's needed because the person might not be ready to hear it.'

A pause. What to say next?

A kookaburra landed on the clothesline, a female, a splash of aqua on its wing feathers.

If the exchange between Dad and me were a research interview, I would have prepared a list of questions. The ethics approval process requires researchers to include in the application what exactly they intend to ask interviewees. And there is a section on the form: 'Will the true purpose of the research be concealed from participants?' It assumes that the ethnographer knows why she has elected to speak with a person, not accounting for the possibility that the true purpose of the research might ambush the researcher herself.

The kookaburra grew perfectly still. We watched it settle its gaze on a corner of the flowerbed, before it nosedived and snatched a small lizard.

What I wanted was a resolution. I wanted some acknowledgment from my father about what it had been like to be his daughter.

I wanted him to say sorry.

Upon realising this, I blushed with shame.

The kookaburra returned to the clothesline and was joined by a mate. They stared at us, and we at them.

'Dad, I've been reading about the Red Army in the 1940s.'

'Why?'

'Because it's your history. It's mine too.'

Silence.

'I've been reading about the Russian soldiers in Berlin and Vienna.'

'You and I cannot possibly sit here in this garden and judge the actions of those soldiers back then,' he said. 'They had seen their friends being blown up, they'd been fed propaganda, they'd been brutalised.'

'Mmm. True. But their revenge was savage.'

Silence.

He shifted in his seat, and I thought he was preparing to stand up, to walk back inside the house, but no, there was a loosening.

'My sister told me we came across a bloated corpse once, though I don't recall this.'

Silence.

'I remember being in our Viennese apartment. The windows had no glass in them, they were papered over. My mother sent my sister and me to get food at the soup kitchen. It was safer for us to go by ourselves than with our young mother. I did not feel afraid. In fact I never felt afraid. I did not have a sense of deprivation. My mother protected my sister and me. For example, we did not go hungry, although I'm sure my mother did. I remember eating army K-rations, gnawing on the large blocks of dark, bitter chocolate. I remember children being rounded up in the neighbourhood by an American soldier and being taken to an ice cream shop, because he'd just won the lottery and wanted to buy them all ice creams.'

More silence.

Then a succumbing.

'What happened, Dad?'

He directed me to switch off the voice recorder.

What he was about to tell me wasn't data. It wasn't testimony to be replayed and catalogued. It was the tentative beginning of a dialogue between parent and child. In the months to come, he would read all this, read my writing, but that would be later. For now, I switched off the recorder, and listened.

*

He was almost two years old in early 1945. Vienna was being bombed. The Red Army was moving west.

His family, like others, was evacuated to a farming hamlet where they joined his grandmother and his aunt and cousin. Supplies were scant. People in the hamlet rationed meals and stored whatever food they had. Russian soldiers advanced in waves. Farmers took it in turns to keep guard through the day and night. Whenever they heard troops coming, they sent out a warning, and the women rushed to the wheat field to hide. Dad's mother, Elizabeth, lay on top of her two children and told them to be quiet. The soldiers stood at the edge of the field and sprayed machine-gun bullets through the golden forage to flush out people. Once, a woman was struck in the buttock by a spent bullet, but she didn't make a sound. Another time, after the soldiers came through during the night, a young wife went looking for her husband in the morning and found his mutilated body.

Soon, Elizabeth stopped hiding in the wheat. Her children's eyes were suffering: they had developed an allergy to the grass. There were other places to disappear to, though.

Soldiers advanced through the apple orchard. Elizabeth called to her children to come to her, but my two-year-old father thought it a game and off he ran. He ran and ran. She ran after him, caught her child and gave him a smack. A soldier witnessed it. He called Elizabeth a bad mother. He took her little son from her and began to walk off with the child, combing the boy's hair with his comb. Elizabeth followed him pleading, 'Give me back my child! Give me back my child!' The man stopped in his tracks, turned to her, and said, 'Okay. I will return him. But only for one hundred eggs.'

The people of the hamlet didn't have a hundred eggs. They raided their cache, surrendering their store, which amounted to several dozen. The soldier ordered that all the eggs be cooked for him. Elizabeth's mother carefully scrambled them and handed over the meal. The man took a few bites. Then he tipped the rest on the ground and urinated all over it. The pile of food lay there, spoiled.

It is false to say that all this is from my father's memory first-hand. He was a toddler and too young to commit entire scenes to his permanent consciousness. The narration was told to him later – and in such a way that cast him as the agent who set in motion the events of that day with the eggs.

Stories are potent things, the ones we mobilise for ourselves, and the ones that are mobilised for us. They give us moral shape. Infants quickly learn the feeling of culpability. Some never learn to shake it. They eventually grow into fathers who ceaselessly find fault in their children.

*

That night I thought about the misplacement of children's guilt, the ease with which stories busily assign individual blame, and yet we are not the sole authors of our lives. Knowing where we came from, the place, the people, is the heartbeat of our telling. When a country resists some sort of nuanced way to talk about its heritage, it leaves its citizens marooned.

My father's country is only now, more than half a century later, acknowledging its National Socialist legacy, its role in the Holocaust. Whereas Germany developed the practice of *Vergangenheitsbewältigung*, the process of overcoming the past, Austria suppressed any examination of the subject. There had almost been a national taboo, Austrian governments and the press remaining in a sort of bubble until eventually they no longer could, for young people began asking brave questions about their grandparents and great-grandparents, and about what had happened.

I was reflecting on all this as I stood in my study at home at night, gazing at the gum trees. 'A stark white ring-barked forest. All tragic to the moon,' Dorothea Mackellar wrote. Beauty, and terror. My own country had yet to find an adequate means to talk about its history; we had no collective way to properly remember – re-member – the place and its inhabitants, what has happened here on this continent to its peoples with the oldest living cultures in the world.

The Australian bush, the rock formations, the skies. The wild oceans, the red desert. I belong to a land that holds in its soil generations of dreaming, and of murder.

28

Jemima turned five. We planned a party with her little friends and cousins at home. She perused the *Women's Weekly* birthday cake book and selected the most complicated design: a Palace of Dreams, with grand stairs and ice-cream cone turrets, a feat of structure and height. My heart sank. Given that I would be preparing the food, plus getting the house in order, there was no way I'd have time to do it. I was directing her towards a plainer style when Brad cut in: 'I'll make it.'

The day before the party, he arrived home early from work with all the requisite candy for decoration, and he set about baking three chocolate loaves. By the time I'd put Jemima to bed, Brad was constructing the castle, cutting out shapes and using skewers and toothpicks to join them together. He'd done engineering at school. His father had been an architect. My husband was no cook – he'd never learnt – but here he was approaching the task as if it were a design model, with astounding success.

We stayed up late coating the palace in butter icing, using blobs as Spakfilla to smooth over lumps and bumps, and had the most fun we'd had in months, adorning the construction with sherbet tiles, piped chocolate windows and marshmallow trees. *I cannot let this marriage die*, I thought.

The next morning we tidied and cleaned and strung balloons around the house, and kids and their parents arrived. The first hour and forty-five minutes proceeded without incident. Then, as Brad carried the cake to the table, a miscommunication between him and me as to who of us was to lead the Happy Birthday song led to a tense exchange. The spectacular castle sat there, everyone admiring it, but we'd sullied the moment. How masterly he and I were at defacing any beauty we created. The celebration concluded, people left. Mindlessly, dejectedly, we both began tidying and cleaning.

Brad and I were an Escher puzzle, a relationship of impossible symmetry. It was so obvious we should work together, I just couldn't see how.

I carried the remains of the Palace of Dreams into the kitchen.

There are an Andes people in South America that have a reverse concept of time. We place the future ahead of us, the past behind; whereas, for the Native Aymara people, the past is ahead of them, the future behind, for they can only ever face what they know and can say for certain happened. This would be a kind of hell, I thought to myself as I scraped cake scraps into the bin. Forever facing the past.

Jemima was flopped in front of a movie. I told Brad we had to talk. He reluctantly followed me into the bedroom, expecting one of our quarrels.

'I want to start over,' I said.

'What do you mean?'

'With you. I want us to start over.'

'Me too,' he said. 'That's what I want.'

'I want to draw a line under everything that's happened, every awful thing we've thought and said to one another, how we've behaved.'

'Yes.'

'That means we need to forgive one another right now. I forgive you. I forgive you for these past few years, for the poison. I love you. And, if we are going to continue, then you need to forgive me too. No more resentment. It's killing us.'

A pause. Brad was regarding me in a new way. My words had penetrated that thick film of whatever it was that usually encased him.

It was the promise of forgiveness. It was the chance to relinquish blame, to give up prior events, to erase consequence. If remorse and regret depend on time for their existence, sometimes grace rests on forgetting.

'I forgive you,' he said, coming over to hug me. 'I love you. And I forgive you.'

29

Over the following months, my nights began assuming a faraway quality. There was a welcome heaviness to my sleep. The more rest I got, the more I required, as adrenaline deserted me and I was left pleasantly wiped out. Often I still woke before dawn, but I'd grown to treasure this hour. Time felt old, slow. I'd brew tea and sit with my notebook, watching the mist in the trees and the lightening of the world, the sky turning blue like a magician's trick.

This tranquillity, if that's what I could call it, was the result of having understood some small part of one's own shape. Gradually I asked Dad more questions, and little by little a picture of my father began to form. Our relationship became a sort of echo, as if in my questions I was saying, *I hear you. I hear what has happened*, and his stories were history's reply.

Forming, too, were tendrils of compassion between Brad and me. On weekends we took the drive east to Mona Vale and wound our way up the coast to Palm Beach, Sydney's northernmost point. The land thinned out there, the headland a pause, a comma. Jemima stood on the jetty at Pittwater and watched the seaplane descend from the heavens, and we played chasings on the sandy tombolo before joining hikers and tourists on the short pilgrimage to the lighthouse at the top of Barrenjoey Head. There were times at home when I caught myself glancing at Brad as he was absorbed in work, and I was reminded that we can't foretell what any of us will or won't do, and that relationships are a mystery. Perhaps this is what is meant by faith, a shadowy tugging of the soul that guides us onwards.

I continued to produce research papers about the justice system, and conducted my final research interview, this one with Judge Solomon, the judge in front of whom David had stood thirty years ago. I was about to leave his chambers when I mentioned David's case: how he had read David's letter and how he'd handed down a suspended sentence. I told him that his decision had changed David's life. Solomon fell quiet before gradually breaking into a smile: 'It's nice to get it right sometimes. Tell him I'm pleased I got it right. And I'm pleased *he* got it right.'

I walked across the park, under the old fig trees, past the Archibald Fountain with its bronze Apollo, and reached St Mary's Cathedral, below which my car was stationed in the car park.

Remorse, guilt, grief, regret and responsibility work upon us in the sharpest and most opaque of ways. Throughout the last several years, I thought I would be able to flush out every wrong-headed thing I'd ever done and might do, as if by doing so I could keep from tripping up; I could keep my daughter safe. I thought I'd be able to identify and categorise my wounds too, all those hurts and slights. If I sought an apology for each thing, pairing every injury with audible statements of penitence, I could achieve chemical neutralisation. Air would be cleared.

I have learnt, though, that remorse need not always be voiced. Sometimes a declaration is required; other times, not, and there exists a moral vanity in indignantly clamouring for spoken words. When a person is truly sorry, sometimes there is no sound at all, simply a softening, and that is enough.

On the stone steps of the cathedral, newlyweds posed for wedding snaps, the photographer crouching low to include the watchful spires touching the sky. The bride's dress was a fairy-tale production, layers of satin and diamantes. At the behest of his boss, the photographer's assistant, a sparrow of a man, held out the bridal veil with the tips of his fingers. *One, two, three!* He let it go, and the thing flew up and outwards, spectre-like, borne by the wind.

*

One Monday, we were given notice on the property we were renting. The owners intended to return earlier than expected, and we had to leave.

Brad and I looked at houses for lease, but with rental prices the way they were, it made sense to buy. I searched real estate sites online, and with each house I asked myself: Could we live there? Would we be happy? Then one evening Jemima was with me on the sofa as I scrolled through photos of prim front lawns, kitchens and living rooms, and when the webpage spontaneously refreshed itself, a new property appeared. She grabbed my arm: 'I want to live *there*.' It was a photo of a long wooden deck nestled among eucalypt treetops. 'It's a *tree house*!' she said. It was around the corner from where we were living. That weekend we walked through the entrance and instantly saw ourselves existing in the space. Three weeks later, Brad and I bought our first home.

We packed our things. We would be going from a capacious four-bedroom house to a compact three-bedder, so we gave away furniture, including Jemima's high chair, pram and cot, and we hired a huge skip and filled it. Brad and I spent a day in the garage sorting through the contents of two-dozen boxes we'd dragged around with us for twenty years. We threw out almost all of it.

On moving day, the removalists arrived early. As they carried everything out to the truck, the three of us took one last look through the rooms in which we'd learnt to be a family.

Our new property is a steep, bushy block. Our house, at the top of a semi-vertical driveway, is built on, and into, rock. The vaulted ceilings, the light and the glass are reminiscent of the property we visited in Tasmania. Our yard is higher still, up another fifteen steps, with a natural rock wall at the back, the ochre of the sandstone glowing in the sun. Jemima sits in the small cave, and is visited by the neighbour's ginger cat that follows her around watching her perform cartwheels and wave at the kids riding bikes on the street below. The land we own is adjacent to a state forest, and from our deck we look out over Sydney blue gums, blackbutts, turpentines, grey ironbarks, and we catch glimpses of understorey shrubs, the wattles and hop bush. Here in this place we somehow possess groundedness and height, a platform for flight.

Brad and I are sharing a study. We are also sharing a bed again. On the night we moved, we lay side by side in our room among stacks of unpacked boxes, and murmured of the future. Then I listened to the pattern of his breathing, and was carried off to sleep.

*

This morning when we woke, it was raining. We heard the delicate beat on the roof, and Jemima's happy patter into our bedroom.

First day of school.

For weeks she'd been asking *when when when* would school start. Now it was here. She shrieked and belly-flopped onto us.

After breakfast, I shimmied her into the checked aqua tunic, the hem settling inches above her ankles, and I stood by while she wrestled with the stiff leather Mary Jane shoes ('*I* can do it, Mum!'), a lump of emotion taking shape in my throat. Then I brushed her hair. When our daughter was born, her hair was black and downy, and we thought it would be dark like mine. She has ended up with my curl – my father's curl – but not the colour. Hers is blonde. I scooped the silky waves into a ponytail.

We walked through wet grass, the air muggy as the rain let up and sunshine materialised, Jemima stooping to wipe water-beads from the tips of her glistening shoes.

Children in the distance filed into the entrance of the local primary school, their broad-brim bottle-green hats a parade of turtles, and when we reached the playground, Jemima's grip on my hand tightened. Scores of mothers and fathers milled around the classrooms, their tiny schoolchildren either bouncing around them, or pressed into their bodies; those parents who, like me, must somehow accept that preparing for loss is not to live.

Four bells sounded, a cheery major triad. Kids whooped and scrambled from their play.

We crept into the 'KB' classroom with its patchwork walls that, by the end of the year, would be crowded with craft, spelling words, self-portraits and science projects. We found her a seat at a table next to an ethereal-looking girl who was drawing castles.

I crouched beside her.

'I love you. Have a wonderful day, darling. I'll pick you up this arvo.'

'Mum. Can you pick me up really, really early?'

'Yes, sweetheart. I'll be right outside the classroom. I'll be there when you walk out.'

'Okay.'

A big breath, now a whisper, her fingers unclasping mine.

'Bye. Go, Mum. You can go.'

Author's Note

To write this book, I relied upon: observations of NSW court hearings between April 2010 and April 2013; observations of NSW private parole meetings and public parole hearings between August 2010 and September 2012; interviews with NSW criminal justice system professionals and other stakeholders, including victims and offenders, between May 2010 and August 2014; court transcripts and judgments; newspaper reports; a body of literary and academic research; as well as my personal journals, and my memory.

When drawing on courtroom dialogue, including judges' judgments, wherever possible I crosschecked such dialogue with official transcripts.

I have opted to use the terms 'offender', 'inmate' and 'prisoner', while recognising that these are contested terms. Many prisoner-rights groups prefer to use 'person convicted of an offence', 'incarcerated person' and 'formally incarcerated person'.

I have changed the names of some individuals.

In some sections, I have used narrative compression.

Sources

Epigraph

vii 'Remorse is memory awake': Emily Dickinson (1924) *The Complete Poems of Emily Dickinson*, Boston: Little, Brown.

Chapter 1

8 'the eighteenth-century neo-classicists attached the term "theatre" to the act of gazing': for a discussion, see Glen McGillivray (2015) 'Arcadian Scenes: Bougainville, Banks and theatrical perception in the South Pacific', in *Embodying Transformation: Transcultural performance*, ed. Maryrose Casey, Melbourne: Monash University Publishing, pp. 1–16.

8 'people have used the language of theatre to describe trial courts': for an exploration of the relationship between performance, truth-telling and the criminal courts, see Kathryn Leader (2007) 'Bound and Gagged: The performance of tradition in the adversarial criminal jury trial', *Philament* 11, pp. 1–20; and Kathryn Leader (2008) *Trials, Truth-Telling, and the Performing Body*, thesis submitted in fulfilment of the requirements for the degree of Doctor of Philosophy, University of Sydney. See also Malcolm Knox (2005) *Secrets of the Jury Room: Inside the black box of criminal justice in Australia*, Sydney: Random House, pp. 190–224.

Chapter 2

13 'all research involving humans observing other humans': see George Devereux (1967) *From Anxiety to Method in the Behavioural Sciences*, The Hague: Mouton & Co., pp. xvi–xx. In using the terms

'tender-minded' and 'tough-minded', Devereux is referring to the work of philosopher William James.

Chapter 3

20 'a conquering gaze from nowhere': Donna Haraway (1990) *Simians, Cyborgs, and Women: The reinvention of nature*, London & New York: Routledge, p. 188.

Chapter 4

34 'to feel remorse for a minor wrong you have committed is to be neurotic': see Michael Proeve & Steven Tudor (2010) *Remorse: Psychological and jurisprudential perspectives*, Surrey & Vermont: Ashgate, p. 42; See also Jeffrie Murphy (2007) 'Remorse, Apology and Mercy', *Ohio State Journal of Criminal Law* 4, p. 430.

Chapter 5

42 'the Warlpiri people in northern Australia who coalesce person and country': see Michael Jackson (1995), *At Home in the World*, Durham, North Carolina: Duke University Press, p. 162.

42 'the Yolmo Sherpa community in Nepal': see Robert Desjarlais (1992) *Body and Emotion: The aesthetics of illness and healing in the Nepal Himalayas*, Philadelphia: University of Pennsylvania Press.

42 'the West's topography of a person as a self-examining, confessing creature': see Michel Foucault (2012, originally published in 1978) *The History of Sexuality, Volume 1: An introduction*, New York: Knopf Doubleday Publishing Group.

Chapter 6

47 'remorse influenced the granting of mercy in death penalty decisions': for a discussion, see Scott Sundby (1998) 'The Capital Jury and Absolution: The intersection of trial strategy, remorse, and the death penalty', *Cornell Law Review* 83, pp. 1557–98.

48 'A law scholar pointed out that, in the moral ordering of convicted offenders': see Richard Weisman (2004) 'Showing Remorse: Reflections on the gap between expression and attribution in cases of wrongful conviction', *Canadian Journal of Criminology and Criminal Justice* 46(2), pp. 121–38.

51 'Viennese society is built on secrets': this is an English translation of a phrase from Emil Bobi (2014) *Die Schattenstadt* (The Void), Austria: Ecowin. The quote appeared in Damien McElroy (2014) 'Vienna really is the espionage capital of the world', *Sydney Morning Herald*, 1 August.

Chapter 7

53 'I was attending local court sessions': for a discussion regarding offence type, seriousness, and the morally sufficient response, see Hannah Maslen (2015) *Remorse, Penal Theory and Sentencing*, Oregon: Hart Publishing, pp. 149–150.

Chapter 8

65 'being reeled in on some ghostly umbilical down the vanished wake of the plane': William Gibson (2003) *Pattern Recognition*, New York: GP Putnam's Sons, p. 1.

67 'it takes existential courage to face the three-fold anxiety of human existence': Paul Tillich (2000, first edition 1952) *The Courage to Be*, New Haven: Yale University, p. 41.

75 'The world is charged with the grandeur of God': see Gerard Manley Hopkins (1995, poem first published 1877) *God's Grandeur and Other Poems*, New York: Dover Publications Inc., p. 15.

Chapter 9

79 'repentance saved their souls': see Bryan S Ward (2006) 'Sentencing without Remorse', *Loyola University Chicago Law Journal* 38, pp. 131–67. See also Jeffrie Murphy (2007) 'Remorse, Apology, and Mercy', *Ohio State Journal of Criminal Law* 4(2), pp. 423–453.

79 'nineteenth-century newspaper articles': the newspaper articles from which the quotes in this chapter are taken are: *Monitor*, 26 November 1827; *Sydney Gazette*, 28 November 1827; *Monitor,* 29 November 1827; *Australian*, 31 December 1827; *Sydney Gazette*, 2 January 1828.

Chapter 11

89 'I read about a 21-year-old man': the details of this case are taken from *Butters v R [2010] NSW CCA 1.*

90 'The judge never heard from him': for a discussion concerning the relationship between offenders' decisions not to give verbal evidence, and

judges' and juries' assessments of offender remorse, see Richard Weisman (2014) *Showing Remorse: Law and the social control of emotion*, Surrey & Vermont: Ashgate, p. 11. See also Susan Bandes (2016) 'Remorse and Demeanor in the Courtroom: Cognitive science and the evaluation of contrition', in *The Integrity of Criminal Process: From theory into practice*, eds Jill Hunter, Paul Roberts, Simon NM Young & David Dixon, Oxford & Portland, Oregon: Hart Publishing, pp. 309–326.

Chapter 13

105 'I might see one hundred matters a day': for a discussion of the workload of magistrates, see Kathy Mack, Sharyn Roach Anleu & Anne Wallace (2011) 'Everyday Work in the Magistrates Courts: Time and tasks', *Journal of Judicial Administration* 21(1), pp. 34–53.

Chapter 14

114 'they must apologise properly': for a discussion regarding the distinction between apology and remorse, see Richard Weisman (2004) 'Showing Remorse: Reflections on the gap between expression and attribution in cases of wrongful conviction', *Canadian Journal of Criminology and Criminal Justice* 46(2), pp.121–138.

Chapter 15

124 'Scientists had recently discovered': for a discussion of the so-called 'crime gene', see Allan McCay (2013) 'Evil Gene Would Make Punishment a Tricky Business', *The Age*, April 22. See also Nicole Vincent ed. (2013) *Neuroscience and Legal Responsibility*, New York: Oxford University Press.

Chapter 17

140 'inmates looked at a split screen': for a discussion of prisoners' experiences of video link technology, see Carolyn McKay (2016) 'Video Links from Prison: Permeability and the carceral world', *International Journal for Crime, Justice and Social Democracy* 5(1), pp. 21–37.

Chapter 19

153 'forgiveness is not a judge's business': Justice Keith Mason, President of the NSW Court of Appeal (2001) 'Forgiving Sin and Punishing Crime', presented at the Lawyers' Christian Fellowship, Brisbane, June 2001.

However, scholar Richard Weisman argues that forgiveness and the law cannot be decoupled (see his paper 'Coupling and Decoupling Remorse and Forgiveness in Legal Discourse'). See also Tracey Booth (2014) 'Victim Impact Statements and the Nature and Incidence of Offender Remorse: Findings from an observation study in a superior sentencing court', *Griffith Law Review* 22(2), pp. 430–55.

155 'enables us to imagine our own reactions in a dark well of horror': Maggie MacKellar (2010) *When It Rains*, Sydney: Vintage, p. 216.

Chapter 23

184 'I know his type of young man': for a discussion of empathy in judicial decision-making, see Susan Bandes (2009) 'Empathetic Judging and the Rule of Law', *Cardozo Law Review de novo*, pp. 133–148.

Chapter 24

191 'In prison, the sort of talk the authorities encouraged': see Maggie Hall & Kate Rossmanith (2016) 'Imposed Stories: Prisoner self-narratives in the criminal justice system in New South Wales, Australia', *International Journal for Crime, Justice and Social Democracy* 5(1), pp. 38–51; for a discussion of people's experiences of their own jail sentences, see Maggie Hall (2017) *The Lived Sentence: Rethinking sentencing, risk, and rehabilitation*, Cham, Switzerland: Springer International Publishing AG.

192 'When she got out of prison': for a discussion concerning the particular needs of women post-release, see Eileen Baldry (2010) 'Women in Transition: From prison to . . .', *Current Issues in Criminal Justice* 22(2), pp. 253–268.

Chapter 25

199 'a disciplined remembrance of the moral significance of what we did': Raimond Gaita (2004, first edition 1991) *Good and Evil: An absolute conception*, Oxford & New York: Routledge, p. 59.

200 'Philosophers called remorse a "retractive" emotion': see Michael Proeve & Steven Tudor (2010) *Remorse: Psychological and jurisprudential perspectives*, Surrey & Vermont: Ashgate, p. 31.

Chapter 26

204 'In his homilies': for his collection of sermons, see Chris Goringe (2014–17) *Creation and Beyond*, Milton Keynes, UK: Lightning Source UK Ltd.

Chapter 27

208 'metaphors are intrinsically nonliteral': Marcus Borg (1998) *The God We Never Knew: Beyond dogmatic religion to a more authentic contemporary faith*, New York: HarperCollins Publishers Inc., p. 58.

212 'we are not the sole authors of our lives': see Michael Jackson's discussions of Hannah Arendt's work in Michael Jackson (2013, originally published in 2002) *The Politics of Storytelling: Violence, transgression and intersubjectivity*, Copenhagen, Demark: Museum Tusculanum Press, p. 18.

212 'My father's country is only now': for an overview of Austria's recent recognition of its past, see Matthew P Berg (2008) 'Commemoration versus *Vergangenheitsbewältigung*: Contextualizing Austria's *Gedenkjahr* 2005', *German History* 26(1), pp. 47–71.

212 'A stark white ring-barked forest. All tragic to the moon': Dorothea Mackellar (2010, poem first published 1908) *My Country*, Malvern, South Australia: Omnibus Books, p. 12.

Acknowledgements

I wish to acknowledge Macquarie University, especially the Faculty of Arts Research Office, for funding and supporting the research for this book.

The research was made possible because of the participation of several hundred people who work in, or who, through circumstance, found themselves involved in, the NSW criminal justice system. I thank all these people for sharing their experiences with me, and for helping facilitate this research, in particular Ian Pike, Martha Jabour, Mark Tedeschi, Robert Cosman, Amy Manuell, Debbie Irons, Bob Inkster and Mindy Sotiri. I acknowledge the cooperation of the NSW courts, and thank the Supreme Court, the District Court, the Local Court, the Coroner's Court, and the Children's Court. I also thank the NSW Parole Authority, the Homicide Victims' Support Group, the Community Restorative Centre, and Legal Aid NSW.

My sincere appreciation goes to Hugh Dillon and Maggie Hall, to whom I consistently turned, and whose legal minds, collegiality and careful reading of my work kept me from being lost at sea. Likewise, to Steven Tudor, Michael Proeve, and Richard Weisman for their conversations and expertise concerning matters of courtroom remorse. Thanks too to Denise Abou Hamad for her research assistance early in the project.

Research is one thing; writing is quite another. In developing *Small Wrongs*, it took me years to develop the story I had to tell, and to tell it. I extend my deepest gratitude to my agent Margaret Connolly for her shrewd guidance, her loving care, and her unshakeable faith in this book and in me as a writer.

I am tremendously grateful to my publisher Arwen Summers for her vision, her astute edits, her warmth and good humour, and I also thank the very wonderful team at Hardie Grant Books. Thank you too to Sandy Cull for the beautiful book cover design.

Earlier versions of some of the writing in this book have appeared in *The Monthly*, *Body & Society*, *TEXT: A journal of writing and writing courses*, *About Performance*, *Australian Feminist Law Journal*, and *International Journal for Crime, Justice & Social Democracy*. I wish to acknowledge the invaluable input I received from those editors and peer reviewers, in particular from John van Tiggelen and the team at *The Monthly*.

My heartfelt thanks go to Peter Doyle, Adrienne Ferreira, Amanda Card, and Glen McGillivray, whose close friendship and counsel I have relied on throughout the writing of this book. To Beth Yahp, who read and provided essential feedback on early drafts, and who discerned the form *Small Wrongs* would take – a memoir – even before I did. Thank you to Margaret Kelly, Nicola Walker, Susan Omundsen, and Betty O'Neill for their camaraderie and thoughtful advice in the early stages of my writing, and to Suzanne Leal for her insightful feedback on my full draft.

I will be forever grateful to Helen Garner: when I was stuck in the middle and ready to abandon the whole thing, her affectionate encouragement kept me going; when I finally reached the other side, her enthusiastic response to my manuscript allowed me to believe that all the suffering was worth it.

Thank you to Professor Michael Jackson for providing feedback at a critical stage, and whose own work proves that combining ethnography with memoir is possible.

Many friends and colleagues supported this project in various ways. In particular I acknowledge Nicole Matthews, Tom Murray, Julie-Anne Long, Karen Pearlman, Kathryn Millard, Willa McDonald, Vanessa Berry, Catharine Lumby, Nicole Anderson, Catriona McKenzie, Joseph Pugliese, Gill Ellis, Jeanette Kennett, Nicole Vincent, Clare Drysdale, Paul Dwyer, Ian Maxwell, Jane Messer, Louise Smith and Iqbal Barkat.

The greatest of love and thanks to my parents, Angela and Gunther, and to my siblings, Julia and Luke, for their generosity and grace while I slowly wrote this book, when I eventually shared drafts with them, and when we talked together. Special thanks to my mum for her endless practical support, and her wisdom, throughout these last eight years.

Lastly, thank you to Brad and Jemima – my heart, my home – who give me the courage to write.